GETTING HELP FROM YOUR DOGS

How to Gain Insights, Advice, and Power Using the Dog Type System

by Gini Graham Scott, Ph.D.
Author of *Do You Look Like Your Dog?*

GETTING HELP FROM YOUR DOGS

Copyright © 2017 by Gini Graham Scott

All rights reserved. No part of this book may be used or reproduced by any means, graphic, electronic, or mechanical, including photocopying, recording, taping or by any information storage retrieval system without the written permission of the author except in the case of brief quotations embodied in critical articles and reviews.

TABLE OF CONTENTS

INTRODUCTION 5
    The Main Categories of Helpers 6
    The Development of this System 6
CHAPTER 1: WHAT'S YOUR DOG? 9
    Determining Your Top Dog, Watch Dog, and Underdog 9
    Discovering Your Top Dog and Watch Dog 10
    Using Guided Meditation or Visualization to Discover Your Top Dog or Watch Dog 12
    Discovering Your Underdog 17
    Working with Your Top Dog, Watch Dog, and Underdog 20
CHAPTER 2: A WORKSHOP ON FINDING YOUR TOP DOG, WATCH DOG, AND UNDERDOG 21
    The Workshop Setting 21
CHAPTER 3: WORKING WITH YOUR DOG 37
    Learning More about Your Dog Family – and You! 37
    Celebrating Your Strengths 46
    Making Your Top Dog and Watch Dog Part of Your Everyday Life 48
    How the Process Works 49
    Getting to Know Your Underdog 52
CHAPTER 4: FIND YOUR INNER GUIDE DOG – OR DOGS 59
    Which Guide Dog Is for You? 59
    Using Your Inner Guide Dog for Different Purposes 60
    Some Exercises to Connect and Communicate with Your Inner Guide Dog 61
    Digging Deep to Find Your Guide Dogs 65
    A Chart to Keep Track of Your Guide Dogs and How They Can Help 68
    Getting the Help You Need 70
    Putting the Advice You Get Into Action 73
    Using the Qualities of Your Guide Dog to Help 74
    Some Examples of Working with Guide Dogs for Help 75

CHAPTER 5: PUTTING ON THE POWER DOG 81
   Why These Exercises Work 81
   Powering Up with Power Animals 82
   A Collection of Power Exercises 84
   To Unleash Your Creativity 87
   Express Yourself More Fully 89
   Increasing Your Energy 90
   Summing Up 92
ABOUT THE AUTHOR 93

INTRODUCTION

The basic Dog Type system is based on understanding more about yourself and others based on the type of dog you and others like the most or least. Or you can imagine what type of dog other people might be, if you don't know their choices for what they like or don't.

It can be helpful to know about the different types of dogs in getting help from your dogs, as described *Discovering Your Dog Type*. This knowledge gives you a greater range of choices and more information about the personality traits of these dogs.

However, you can still gain help from different dogs based on what you already know about the most popular dogs. For example, you probably already know about Beagles, Dachshunds, German Shepherds, Golden Retrievers, Boxers, Pit Bulls, Collies, Labradors, Poodles, and other dogs you read about every day. And if you own a dog, you know a lot about that breed or mix, as well as other dogs you learned about before deciding on the dog you finally got.

The way to get help is to use your power of visualization to call on different types of dogs for different purposes. The process is similar to using meditation, hypnosis, journeying, or other techniques to tap into your intuition or inner creative force – however you want to call it. In using these techniques in different systems, you may call on teachers, guides, helpers, mentors, coaches, gurus, heroes, spirits, wise men or women, or the image of real people you admire. The difference in the Dog Type system is that you are calling on different types of dogs you associate with different abilities and powers for their help.

The Main Categories of Helpers

There are six main categories of dogs you can call on, and you choose the breed of dog to provide that kind of help you need. These categories are:

Guide Dogs, who are like mentors or wise men or women in that they provide you with advice.

Power Dogs, who you imagine as being very strong, assertive, and powerful; you gain power and confidence from them.

Top Dogs, who are your favorite dogs; you look to them as family members, relatives, or friends, who can share their insights, wisdom, and support with you.

Watch Dogs, who provide you with protection, such as in a scary situation, to help you overcome your fears and warn you to avoid danger.

Underdogs, who represent the things you don't like, including your weaknesses or lack of abilities in some area; you can acknowledge or seek to change and improve them.

Rescue Dogs, who can help you out of difficult situations, when you need some extra help.

The Development of this System

As described in more detail in *Discovering Your Dog Type,* this approach of calling on your dogs developed out of a series of workshops I conducted, based on using the dog profiles to find different dogs for these six types of help. Alternatively, you can use the dogs you already know about to call on for different types of help.

I have included examples of these workshops to illustrate how participants used the Guide Dogs, Power Dogs, Top Dogs, and other types of dogs to help them in everyday situations. As these examples show, the Dog Type system can be a powerful method you can use regardless of any other spiritual, religious, or self-help system you are involved with. Just think of your dogs as an alternate source of help you can draw on in your personal or work life. Also, you can use this system in a group to gain insights about yourself from both your dogs and from others in the group.

This approach is not only designed to provide you with the help you need, but it is designed to be fun. It is designed to be a lighthearted way to use these techniques to get the needed information and help. So feel free to supplement these exercises and visualizations with fun objects, or combine seeking insights with other things you enjoy doing. For example, call on your dogs while you take a walk in your neighborhood, hike on a nature trail, enjoy a cruise, or have dinner in a trendy restaurant.

In other words, you can use this system anywhere and at any time. For example, if you are at a social gathering or at a meeting, you can take a few moments to call on your Guide Dog for advice about what to do or say in a particular situation. If you are going to a job interview or important meeting, you can call on your Power Dog to watch over you and give you an infusion of power and confidence. If you are nervous about doing something you haven't done before – such as speaking to a large audience – you can ask your Rescue Dog to help you overcome your anxiety.

So get ready, get set, and learn how different kinds of dogs can help you succeed at whatever you are doing. And if you wish, use the Dog Profiles to help you choose the dogs to help you – or select your helpers from the dogs you already know about.

CHAPTER 1: WHAT'S YOUR DOG?

Just as the expression: "What's your sign?" refers to one of 12 astrological signs and "What's your type?" refers to one of 16 Myers-Briggs personality types, "What's your dog type?" refers to the dog profile you most identify with.

The dog you like the most or feel the most connection with is your "Top Dog." Your second favorite is your "Watch Dog" or "Guard Dog," since it's next in line, like a body guard to the Top Dog. These two dogs represent who you are now or would like to be.

Last, and in this case least, is the dog you like the least or feel the least connection with. This is your "Underdog," which has the traits you don't have – or don't want to have.

You can use the Dog Profile descriptions in *Discovering Your Dog Type* as a guide with more information on different breeds of dogs. Or select from the dogs you already are familiar with. It doesn't matter if you own a dog or not.

Determining Your Top Dog, Watch Dog, and Underdog

If you already own a dog, this may turn out to be your Top Dog or Watch Dog, particularly if you have given much thought to choosing the dog you own, which is the case for many people who show their dogs at dog shows. They spend hours poring through dog books, visiting dog breeders, talking to other owners of that breed, and carefully selecting the breed they want to raise and show. After joining the dog show circuit, they become part of a close community of owners of that breed. So commonly, their Top Dog choice is already clear.

In other cases, the dog you own may not necessarily be your Top Dog or Watch Dog, such as if you got your dog as a gift or adopted a dog that wandered into your yard. Also, your dog might be an unlikely contender, if your dog is very unlike you, such as if you are a high-energy go-getter, and your dog grows from a playful pup into a lazy dog that loves to spend the day curled up on your couch.

How do you determine your Top Dog, Watch Dog, and Underdog? The following chapter describes the process and how to use that information to learn more about yourself and for personal and professional development. You can additionally use that information to better understand and relate to others and achieve greater success.

So let's get started on the "Dog Trail", so to speak, to learn more about you.

Discovering Your Top Dog and Watch Dog

There are several ways to determine your Top Dog and Watch Dog. Use whichever method is most applicable for you, or use two or more methods to help confirm your choice. You can repeat the process from time to time, since your choices can change over time, as you change your dog type preferences or identifications. Such changes often occur when you work on personal and professional development. In fact, to make changes in your life, change your Top Dog to help you refocus on the traits you want to develop – and gradually you will become more like that dog.

If your first and second choices have the same Dog Type Profile, such as if a Beagle is your first choice and a Basset Hound is your second choice, that's like having one astrological sign — say Gemini — for both your birth and rising sign, which makes you a "Double Gemini." The same goes for choosing your dog type. If your choices are similar, that shows that this profile is even more clearly your type.

Here are the major ways to identify your dog choices.

1) <u>You already own a dog and know that's the dog for you</u>. So that's your Top Dog. Then, go on and choose your Watch Dog.
2) <u>Review the Dog Type Profiles</u> and choose the one you might like or most identify with as your Top Dog; your next favorite is your Watch Dog. If you have already chosen your Top Dog, review the dog profiles again to make your second choice. As you glance through the pictures, make your choice based on your first impression or "top of mind" reaction. Later, you can read through the "What's Your Personality and Style?" or "Little Bit of History" section to get more acquainted with that breed. As you learn more about these different types of dogs, feel free to change your Top Dog or Watch Dog. (For example, say you decide that a gentle herder like an English Sheep Dog is too soft and cuddly, and you prefer to identify with a more aggressive hunter dog. Make the change.)
3) <u>Use a guided meditation or visualization to choose your dog</u>. To use this method, you will get very relaxed and meditate or take a journey by yourself, with a partner, or in a group. Before doing so, review the Dog Type Profiles on your own or in a group for an overview of the different dog types. Or make a list of the different dogs you are familiar with. Then, use meditation or a visualization to make your final choice, based on strongly feeling a preference, identification, or connection with your favorite dog.

Whichever method you choose, first select your Top Dog, and then your Watch Dog. Should you use a guided meditation or visualization to make your choice, here are a few approaches you might use. Choose the method that feels most comfortable for you.

Using Guided Meditation or Visualization to Discover Your Top Dog or Watch Dog

Take some time to think about the different types of dogs, before beginning to meditate or visualize, unless you are confirming a choice you have already made. It's best not to make a choice in advance, since doing this can skew your experience, so you are drawn to an already made choice. Rather, use this initial review to think about the range of dogs that exist.

When you review the breed profiles or make a list of familiar breeds, don't expect to remember all of the dogs in detail, since your conscious mind normally cannot process and categorize so much information. But as you do your review to find your Top Dog and Watch Dog, your unconscious mind will pick up the types of dogs you feel especially drawn to. Then, when you meditate or use visualization, this unconscious information will be available to you, since you are in a very relaxed, focused state of mind where you can tap into your unconscious.

To get acquainted with the different types of dogs, spend about 10-15 minutes doing a Dog Type Profile review or making your list of familiar dogs. Look at the profiles or your list. If you use the profiles, notice the dog names and photos and read the profile descriptions. If you have time, look at the historical descriptions. Then, use one of the following techniques to get in this altered state and choose your two favorite dogs.

Using Meditation or Reflection to Find Your Top Dog or Watch Dog

For this technique, first use the Dog Type Profiles you have reviewed or the list you have created. Place the profiles section or your list before you. Have some stick-on notes available to help you narrow down your choices.

Next, get in a very relaxed, reflective state by focusing on your breathing going in and out or staring ahead in an unfocused way for a minute or two.

Then, with the goal of looking for your "Top Dog" in mind, go back through the profiles or you list. Gaze one each profile in an unfocused way. You can also combine unfocused looking with putting your palm over that page or name on your list and feeling if you get a warm or cool sensation or feel a vibration. Then, listen to your inner voice tell you "Yes or No" or go by the sensation you feel – warm or a vibration for "Yes", cool or no vibration for "No". Mark the "Yeses" with a post-it note.

If you have more than one "Yes" selected, go through the process again with those "Yeses." This time, with your goal of seeking your "Top Dog" in mind, ask for an even stronger "Yes," warmer sensation, or stronger vibration. Once more eliminate any "Nos."

Continue this process until you end up with a single "Yes." That is your Top Dog.

To choose your Watch Dog, go back to your last selection of "Yeses." If there is just one other dog selected, that is your Watch Dog. If there is more than one, go through this process one last time to end up with a single "Yes." This is your Watch Dog — your second favorite choice.

Taking a Dog Walk to Find Your Top Dog or Watch Dog

This approach to finding your dog involves doing a visualization where you take a walk through a dog park to meet your Top Dog and then your Watch Dog. Be generally familiar with the different types of dogs or dog profiles before you start visualizing. Get relaxed and use the following visualization as a guide – or record it and play it back as you listen. Or in a group, one person can read this, while others have the experience.

Imagine that you are going into a dog park with a walking trail through a woods and meadow to a large lake. The dog park is a place where dogs can run free and off the leash. It is a bright, sunny day, as you drive into the parking lot, park, and walk into the dog park.

As you walk in, you see a large open area where many dogs are exercising and playing, while their owners are off to the side, watching. The dogs are running, jumping, cooling off in tubs of water, chasing through tunnels, and having a great time.

Watch the dogs for a while, feeling very comfortable and relaxed as you do. Then, you notice a trail off to the side of the park, and you head toward it, so you can meet the dog you like most or most identify with. This will be your Top Dog.

Now start walking on the trail. It winds around and goes into the woods. As you walk along through the trees, you notice some dogs appear on the side of the trail. They may be some dogs you saw playing before, or some new dogs. If they look at you, just smile at them and notice if any of them seem especially interested in you. Possibly your Top Dog may be among them, or maybe not. Continue to walk on to find your Top Dog.

Then, you come to an open meadow with a few scattered trees. You notice a number of dogs running around and playing there. They may be some of the dogs you saw playing before or some new dogs. Stop for a short time to observe. Notice if you seem to be especially drawn to or interested in some of these dogs and focus on observing them. If they look at you, smile at them and notice if any seem especially interested in you. Possibly your Top Dog may be among them, or maybe not.

Continue to walk on. Now you will come to a lake. This is where you will find your Top Dog. Go over to the lake and sit down on the bank and look into the water. Ask for the dog you like the most or feel the most identification with to appear. As you ask that question, your Top Dog will appear beside you to your right, and you'll see its face appear in the water. Should you see more than one dog there, notice which one you feel most drawn to and invite that dog to stay. Then, the others will leave and return to the meadow.

Now, turn to your Top Dog and take some time to get acquainted and make a connection with that dog. You can shake its paw, pet it. Then, talk to it. Ask it some questions about what it likes and doesn't like, and what activities it prefers. Notice the ways in which you are similar to that dog, such as in personality and appearance. Think about the things you especially like about that dog or why you feel the most identification with it. Consider the reasons you might feel the greatest connection with that dog; why you have chosen it to be your Top Dog – or maybe why it has chosen you.

Take a few minutes to reflect on these questions, and as you do, feel your connection with your Top Dog growing. Know that you can always turn to it for help, as well as any other dogs you might call on for assistance.

Then, with your Top Dog still seated beside you, look back into the water. Now ask for the dog you like next most or feel the next most identification with to appear there. As you ask that question, your Watch Dog will appear beside you on your left, and you'll see its face appear before you in the water. If your Watch Dog is the same breed as your Top Dog, that's fine. It just means you have an especially strong preference for or identification with that dog. Should you see more than one dog, notice which one you feel most drawn to and invite that dog to stay. Then, the others will leave and return to the meadow.

Now, turn to your Watch Dog and take some time to get acquainted and make a connection with that dog. Consider this dog your Top Dog's helper or companion. You can shake its paw, pet it. Then, talk to it. Ask it some questions about what it likes and doesn't like; and what activities it prefers. Notice the ways in which you are similar to that dog, such as in personality and appearance. Think about the things you especially like about that dog or why you feel the next most identification with that dog. Consider the reasons you have chosen it to be your Watch Dog – or maybe why it has chosen you.

Take a few minutes to reflect on these questions, and as you do, feel your connection with your Watch Dog growing. Know that you can always turn to it for help, as well as any other dogs you might call on for assistance.

Then, with these two dogs still beside you, feel their strength and power. Think of them as reflecting different aspects of yourself and as helpers that will teach you more about yourself, so you more clearly see who you are now and who you want to be. Also, know that you can always come back here to communicate with them – or you can always call on them when you want them to appear wherever you are so you can talk to them.

Now take a few minutes to say your "Goodbyes" and let them know you plan to contact them again. Then, turn and head back along the trail. Walk through the meadow and woods and then back into the dog park. Finally, walk back to your car to go home. As you walk, you feel very confident and secure now that you have found your Top Dog and Watch Dog, who you can turn to for more insights about yourself, as well as advice on what to do in different situations.

Working with Your Top Dog and Watch Dog

Now that you know your Top Dog and Watch Dog, you can work with this information to learn more about yourself, as well as think about what you might want to change and further develop in yourself. You can additionally work with these dogs as Inner Guide Dogs or Power Dogs, turning to them for advice or extra power in different areas of your life, as discussed in subsequent chapters.

When you change through this process, you may find yourself drawn to different Top Dogs and Watch Dogs. That's because the changes you make may lead you to prefer or identify with different dogs. So from time to time, check to see if you still have the same Top Dog and/or Watch Dog. If not, reflect on what this new Top Dog or Watch Dog has to tell you about yourself and where you might develop next.

Once you use this knowledge to learn more about yourself, you can apply this system to learn more about others and improve your relationships with them by determining or imagining their Top Dogs, Watch Dogs, and Underdogs, as will be described in a later chapter in more detail. For now, focus on learning to use the system for yourself.

Discovering Your Underdog

While your Top Dog and Watch Dog represent who you are or would like to be, your Underdog has qualities you don't have or don't want. Here's how to meet your Underdog. You use a first impression, guided meditation or journey, or both, much like you found your Top Dog and Watch Dog.

Using Meditation or Reflection to Find Your Underdog

For this technique, as in finding your Top Dog and Watch Dog, use the Dog Type Profiles or your list of dogs you have created. Place the chapter of the book with these profiles or your list before you, and eliminate from consideration your Top Dog and Watch Dog. Once more, get in a very relaxed, reflective state.

Now, with the goal of looking for your Underdog in mind — the dog you like the least or least identify with, go back through the profiles or your list. As you turn each page or look at each name, gaze at the profile or listing in an unfocused way. As before, notice if you get a warm or cool sensation or vibration from the listing of that dog and listen to your inner voice telling you "Yes" or "No," until you feel a strong "Yes" or "No" sensation. Once you end up with a single "Yes," that's your Underdog – the dog you least prefer or least identify with.

Going to the Dog Pound to Find Your Underdog

This approach involves using visualization to visit the dog pound to meet your Underdog. You should already be familiar with different types of dogs and their profiles, since you have used them to find your Top Dog and Watch Dog. The dog pound metaphor is used, since this is where you find many rejected dogs in cages, unlike going to a dog park to find your Top Dog and Watch Dog, because there you will find dogs off leash, exercising, and running free. So now get ready to find your Underdog at the pound.

Imagine that you are going to the dog pound located in the downtown or industrial area of your city. The pound is filled mostly with unwanted dogs that have been given away by their owners. Others have been lost or are strays. They're in separate cages, and most are bored, angry, or sad at being there.

You arrive at the pound, knowing that you are looking for your Underdog, the dog you like the least or feel the least connection with. Once you find it, you can release it from the pound, so you can meet with it for its help in learning more about yourself.

Once you arrive, park and go in. Inside, you see the pound director, who will take you on a walk through the pound. As you walk, notice the dogs in the cages on either side. They look at you with interest. Some jump up and down in their cages, eager to get out and join you. Others bark, wanting to show their anger at being in a cage.

Should you see any dogs that look like your Top Dog or Watch Dog, that's fine. Just pass them by, knowing they will not be your Underdog, too. They just happen to be in the pound.

Keep on walking. Make a complete circuit of the pound, so you see all of the dogs there. Then, go back to look for your Underdog, and as you walk around, notice which dog you like the least or feel the least connection with. You may notice that the dog senses this by withdrawing as you go by. Or maybe it will bark to let you know that you seem like an unwelcome stranger.

If so, this might be your Underdog, though keep walking around the pound to be sure. As you walk around, notice if there is another dog you don't like or feel little or no connection with. If so, go around again and choose the dog where you feel the least liking or connection. This is your Underdog.

Now that you know your Underdog, it's time to make some connection. So go back to that dog's cage and stand there trying to relate to it. Take some time to get acquainted. You may feel hesitant at first, but as you stand there, the dog feels more and more calm and comfortable with you. Then, you can shake its paw, pet it, and talk to it. Ask it some questions about what it likes and doesn't like; what activities it prefers. Notice the ways in which you are different from that dog, such as in personality and appearance. Think about the things you especially don't like about that dog or why you feel the least identification with that dog. Consider why you have chosen it to be your Underdog – or maybe why it has chosen you.

Take a few minutes to reflect on these questions. As you do, feel your connection with your Underdog growing, even though you still like it the least or feel little or no identification with it. For you have much you can learn from it.

To continue to learn from your Underdog, take that dog out of the pound. Take it with you on a leash or in your arms to your car. Next, take it with you to the dog park. As you release it, it is very happy in this new place and will be glad to meet with you again here or come to your house if you prefer. You can then turn to it for more information about yourself and for insights into the qualities you want to eliminate in yourself and how to do so.

Finally, see your Underdog run off, turn away and leave the dog park, knowing you can always call on your Underdog for more insights about yourself.

Working with Your Top Dog, Watch Dog, and Underdog

Now that you've discovered your Top Dog, Watch Dog, and Underdog, you're ready to work with them to learn more about yourself and the qualities you want to further develop, change, or eliminate. In the process, you'll want to get to know them, too, because as you know more about them, you'll learn more about you. Just check the dog's profile or what you know about the dog to do so.

To illustrate different ways of working with these dogs, the next chapter features a workshop with a group of people who experienced the process of finding their Top Dog, Watch Dog and Underdog.

CHAPTER 2: A WORKSHOP ON FINDING YOUR TOP DOG, WATCH DOG, AND UNDERDOG

In the previous chapters, I described how to find your Top Dog or favorite dog, Watch Dog or next favorite, and Underdog, the dog you like the least. Before discussing how to work with these choices to better understand yourself, here's an example from a small workshop I conducted with a dozen people. This illustration will also provide a guide for setting up your own small group.

With a larger group, after people pick their dogs, I recommend getting them into groups with similar choices to participate in various exercises and discussions together. In this case, everyone sat in one group, made their choice and later discussed their experience. I changed the identities and descriptions of the participants for confidentiality. Here's how I described the workshop.

The Workshop Setting

I used a relaxed, comfortable setting – a large room in my house with soft carpeting, large pillows, and low lighting. Everyone took off their shoes and sat around in a circle on the pillows.

I began with a brief introduction to the Dog Type system and what would happen tonight: they would meet their Top Dog, Watch Dog, and Underdog, and discover what they could learn from and about themselves. Holding up a picture of the Dog Star Chart to illustrate, I explained:

"This is the Dog Type system. If you're familiar with astrology, this is what the basic system looks like. It's divided into 4 sections that represent the major areas of personality — power, energy, social skills, and individual traits. Then these are further divided so there are 12 main dimensions. The different types of dogs can be profiled on these dimensions, which are like spokes on a wheel.

The basic underlying principle is that the kinds of dogs you are drawn to reflect your personality and lifestyle. The dogs you don't like reflect the characteristics you don't have or don't like in yourself, and you'd like to get rid of. I've combined the most important dogs into families of dogs, and dog profiles of the chosen dogs.

What we'll do tonight is look at how you connect to your Top Dog, which is your favorite dog or the dog you prefer or relate to the most. Then, we'll look at your second favorite dog, which is your Watch Dog. Finally, you'll meet the dog you like the least, and called appropriately the Underdog.

You'll see all of the dog profiles in this booklet of dog types. Look through it. Get a sense of the different types of dogs and those you feel a kinship with. Then, we'll do a visualization to find your Top Dog and Watch Dog. Then, we'll look at how you relate to your Top Dog and Watch Dog and discuss the qualities they have and the qualities you might like to develop."

Next, before starting the exercises, I asked the participants to describe a little about themselves and what they hoped to gain from the workshop. The participants also spent time talking about their dogs, since they were dog owners and their dogs were very important to them.

Among the participants were Andrew, a marketing sales rep; Flo, an elementary school teacher; Susan, an administrative assistant; Heddy, a retired secretary; Jim, a Web designer; and Paul, a supervisor at a manufacturing company. Here are some of their comments, to give a flavor of these introductions. Interestingly, the initial dog descriptions provided a context for the later discussions of how they felt a kinship with their chosen dogs

–sometimes the same as a dog they owned, but more generally a different type of dog.

Susan, emphasized the importance of giving her dog, an Arctic German Shepherd, instructions, and trusting him as a protector, qualities that led her to choose it as her Top Dog, too. As she described her dog:

> "I have an Arctic German Shepherd, and we are very bonded. I like her because she listens well and follows instructions. She knows if she's done something I don't like, even before I get to the area where she might have destroyed something. But mostly, she's a good dog and gets along well. If she's done something bad, she'll run to her bed and cover her head to let me know there's something wrong. She doesn't go outside much, because in my neighborhood, there are pit bulls, which are trained for fighting."

Flo, the teacher, emphasized the importance of her Rottweiler/German Shepherd Mix being both gentle with children and a good protector, noting that he won't let anybody come in the yard that he doesn't know."

Andrew spoke about his own Rottweiler being very aggressive, yet with a gentle disposition and easy to train. "He's like a big baby, and very intelligent. He listens to everything I tell him. I found him on the street and he's a good dog, very dependable, very protective. He likes to please you and is easily trainable." He also praised his second dog, a "very protective, really mellow" German Shepherd Mix. "Her name is Patience and she has a lot of patience, though she has a little evil side which comes out when she sees a dog on the street and begins barking and lunging. But basically she is a good dog and minds very well. I use treats and can train both my dogs to do anything." One reason he had for attending the workshop was that he hoped to learn why he was drawn to the big dogs, as well as learn more about the dogs he didn't like and why.

The others similarly described a little about themselves and what they hoped to learn. I handed out booklets with the dog profiles. Then I invited the participants to glance through the booklets to get familiar with the different types of dogs, since the dogs they chose as their favorites might not be the dog they owned, and they didn't need to own a dog. As I explained:

"What I'd like to do now is give you these Dog Profile Books, so you can look at the various types of dogs to help you choose your Top Dog, Watch Dog, and Underdog. Don't try to make your choice now. Just use the book to get familiar with these dogs, since the dog you choose could be the dog you own or it could be another dog you feel a kinship with."

While they looked at the pictures of dogs, I put on the What Kind of Dog Are You? theme song – a humorous song about why people choose the dogs they do to provide some lighthearted background music to keep the mood light and upbeat. In your own workshops, you can use whatever background music you like, or nothing at all.

Here's a copy of the What Kind of Dog Are You? song that was inspired by creating the Dog Type. You can download a copy of the song from the WhatsYourDogType.com website.

WHAT KIND OF DOG ARE YOU?[1]

CHORUS If someone asked you, what would you say?
What kind of dog are you?
Are you more like a toy,
A bundle of joy,
Or a rough tough mutt through and through?

---

[1] Copyright Gini Graham Scott 2003; Lyrics and Music by Gini Graham Scott

VERSE   Take Joe with a mastiff.
           He works as a bailiff.
           Tough guy in the courts and in life.
           Don't push him around,
           Or he'll run you aground.
           With the help of his bulldog-like wife.

VERSE   Now look at sweet Cherise.
           She chose a Pekingese.
           Loves to preen and show off in style.
           Has the same look-at-me walk.
           Same perked ears when she talks.
           Both seek love like the Queen of the Nile.

CHORUS 2   So if someone asked you, what would you say?
           What kind of dog are you?
           Are you more like a Chow,
           That's built like a cow?
           Are you more like a Hound,
           Your nose to the ground?
           Or a Whippet, like a bolt from the blue?

VERSE   And then there's old Pete,
           Found his dog on the street.
           A mutt from a long line of strays.
           Both lazy and laid back.
           Yet fight hard if attacked.
           Their pedigree: a great love of play.

BRIDGE   So the answer seems clear.
           Your choice shows who you are.
           The dog you like the most
           Is like a sign up on a post.

FINAL So what kind of dog are you?
CHORUS Yeah, what kind of dog are you?
If someone asked you, what would you say?
What kind of dog are you?

After the song ended, I explained that we would now do a guided fantasy meditation, so everyone should get comfortable, and I would lower the lights. Then, I explained the process of going to a dog park to find their Top Dog, Watch Dog and Underdog.

"You'll be taking a walk to find your Top Dog and Watch Dog. Then, we'll talk a little about that and next you'll find your Underdog. After that, we'll look at ways you can work with these dogs. We'll use this meditation where you go to the dog park to make your choice."

Now, with everyone relaxed and comfortable, I used the Dog Park guided experience, after about 30 seconds of introductory comments. I began by telling everyone, "Now concentrate on your breathing going in and out, in and out, feeling very calm and relaxed, yet alert and aware, so you hear the sound of my voice," to calm everyone and get them receptive to the experience. Then, I slowly read the guided experience.

The experience lasted for about 7 minutes, and was like going to a movie, which the participants created in their mind, as I led them along the trail in the Dog Park through a woods, to a meadow, and then to a lake, where they saw the reflection of their Top Dog, and then their Watch Dog, seated on either side of them.

Afterward, I used a short commentary to bring them back – "Now I'm going to count from 5 to 1, and as I do, you'll come back into the room:5, 4, you're becoming more awake and alert; 3, 2; More and more alert and awake; And 1, you're back in the room.

Once everyone was back, I asked them: "How did that feel? What did you experience?" Then everyone in turn described how they had met their Top Dog and Watch Dog. Afterward, I asked some follow-up probing questions about how the qualities of their Top Dog or Watch Dog reflected their own qualities.

For example, here's my exchange with Andrew, who reported that he was drawn to two big dogs – a Collie and a St. Bernard, though neither was the same as the Rottweiler and German Shepherd Mix he currently owned.

Andrew: "I was attracted to the Collie type of dog."

GGS: "What was it about the Collie that appealed to you?"

Andrew: "Because it seemed like a peaceful dog. Mellow."

GGS: "Are those qualities you feel you have or would like to develop more?"

Andrew: "I feel I have those peaceful qualities. I think I'm a little mellow."

GGS: "And what was your second dog?"

Andrew: "My second dog was a St. Bernard."

GGS: "What was it about the St. Bernard that appealed to you?"

Andrew: "The strongness and the bigness. He's big, but he doesn't have to use it. It's like his bigness gives him that assurance and confidence."

GS: "The St. Bernard is also known as a protective and loyal dog, and he's a well-known rescue dog. Would you say those kind of qualities describe you?"

Andrew: "Yes, loyal I think, because I really stay committed to other people I know and trust. And I think the rescue part fits me, because I'm always trying to help people."

Likewise, Flo felt a strong resemblance between the Golden Retriever she selected as her Top Dog and herself. She was especially impressed by the Golden Retriever's gentle, lovable qualities, combined with being an easy dog to train. Similarly, she had a very gentle, quiet, warm, friendly manner about her, coupled with an eagerness to do things that people asked of her most of the time. For her Watch Dog, she chose a German Shepherd, because of its qualities as a strong, trainable protector. Here are the highlights of my exchange with her.

GGS: "Flo, what was your experience?"

Flo: "I picked a Golden Retriever."

GGS: "What was it about the Golden Retriever that you especially liked?"

Flo: "They're gentle, though they can be aggressive, and they're very lovable. They're an easy dog to get along with and easy to train."

GGS: "Would you say those are qualities that you have, too?"

Flo: "Definitely."

GSS: "What about your second dog?"

Flo: "I would say a German Shepherd. I like those dogs because they are good watchdogs, good with children, easy to get along with, and very trainable. Once you train them, they'll be a real good housedog. And once you train them and tell them what to do, they just do it."

GGS: "Would you say that about yourself, that you're good at being trained, say by taking instructions when people instruct you?"

Flo: "Yeah, I'm good at doing things people ask me to do. Sometimes whether I want to do it or not, I just do it."

At this point, Flo's friend, Andrew, who had invited her to the workshop, also had his own insights about the good match between Flo and her Top Dog.

Andrew: "And Flo's real loyal. Definitely. When she says she's going to do something, she does it."

Flo: "Almost do or die."

GGS: "That's very true of German Shepherds. They're excellent at doing what their owner wants, and you associate that with them. They're police dogs and watchdogs, because they're really good about following orders. You train them not to bark, to be nice to people, and they do that, such as when the police use the dog to help them catch a criminal and then take it to school with them to meet and greet the kids."

Flo strongly agreed that shepherd dogs are so well behaved. "You can tell them: 'Lie down over there and stay there till I get back', and you get back, and they're still there. They're doing exactly what you asked them to do."

Then Susan explained why she chose an Arctic German Shepherd, the same dog she owned, because of the qualities of trust and dependability, though the dog sometimes acted as a surrogate for her in expressing her anger toward several neighbors, she described as "bad actors". Then, too, the dog had the same pugnacious, tenacious qualities, she had in going after what she wanted or felt was right. As Susan described her experience:

"Regardless of how I feel, if she wants something done, she'll keep walking back and forth, looking at me, until I eventually get up, which she wants.

"I like her because she's very trustworthy, she's dependable, I don't worry when I leave my house about somebody coming in that she doesn't know. I also like her because I live in an apartment, behind my garage, and she lets me know as soon as somebody pulls up if it's somebody she knows. Then she'll go "aaaah....aaaah" and run back and forth to let me know that. But if it's somebody she doesn't know, she'll bark and won't leave the door until I come to see who it is.

"And what I really like is her toughness, such as one night when my neighbor threw some charcoal in the backyard, when I was asleep. I kept hearing her bark, and she wouldn't lie down. Then, when I saw her running back and forth in the street, I realized something was wrong. So when I got up, the garage was on fire behind me, and she kept barking until she made sure I got up. So I know that I can count on her. She's trustworthy, she's lovable, and she's stubborn."

GGS: "Would you say those characteristics go for you, too?"

Susan: "Yeah. They are."

Then, Susan described her second choice, a Cocker Spaniel, again emphasizing the importance of trust and persistence. Plus she liked its sensitive nature and felt she had these same qualities, explaining:

"My second choice was the Cocker Spaniel, because they are so cute, and I believe they are trustworthy and loyal, which is very important to me.

"Plus if they like you they like you, and if they don't, they don't. And I'm like that, too. I either like people or I don't, and I show them just where they stand. If I like you, I'll open up my heart to you, and if not, I'm like, 'Get out of my face.'"

Then, Heddy described her choices, which were dogs she previously or currently owned. She was drawn to her first dog, a Cocker Spaniel, because she not only liked its playfulness – a quality she shared too, but she felt it was very protective, and realized that she was generally protective of other people. She liked the Rottweiler next, because it was a tough dog that helped her in putting up a stronger shield against other people she didn't want in her life. As she explained:

"I chose a Cocker Spaniel for my first dog, because I used to have a Cocker Spaniel and liked her very much. For one thing, I like to play with my dog, so she was perfect for me, because she was always very playful. Plus I liked that she was very protective, a good watchdog. I feel I am protective of other people, as well.

"And what I liked about the Rottweiler is he's protective about me outside. I'll go inside the house, and if he doesn't like somebody, he'll show that, which is good because of the neighborhood I'm in. Many people are phony or mean, such as the man next door. The man calls him "dirty dog", and he doesn't like that man either. And he shows how he really feels to my neighbor and his kids who come over and throw things at him. So he doesn't like these kids either. And he shows what I'd like to express myself. He shows what he thinks of him by going by his edge of the yard."

Nancy, who picked a Terrier, a dog she already owned, described how both she and her dog shared a similar memory for past slights and mistreatments, and never forgot. As she commented:

> "When my dog was a little puppy, this friend of mine teased her, and to this day, she remembers that. For example, one day when he had to use my bathroom, he told me my dog was lying right in front of the door to block him from going in. My dog was there, because she never forgot what he did when she was younger. And like me, she's like that with anybody who ever mistreated her; she doesn't fool with them. She's very sensitive. Another example is I have a neighbor across the street who comes over to work in my garage. Once he hit her with a hammer, and now if he comes anywhere near her, my dog tries to bite him. So it shows that you cannot tease or mess with my dog and then expect to go anywhere near her.
>
> "And I won't forget either. If somebody treats me badly, I don't want to be bothered with them anymore. I don't take it, just like my dog won't. For example, that happened once with my own boss, who tried to do me in. She first tried to keep me from getting another job. Then, she called the police and child protective services claiming I abused my son, who has some mental disabilities, but it wasn't true. And whenever my dog sees her, she just growls at her and threatens to attack. She knows she's no good."

Once everyone had explored their connection with their Top Dog and Watch Dog, the next step was for each person to go to the dog pound to meet their Underdog. I thought this was an appropriate place to find this dog, since the pound is a place for cast-off and unwanted dogs.

Using another guided fantasy meditation, I led them through a pound to choose their Underdog from the caged dogs there, using the Dog Pound exercise described in Chapter 4. Afterward, I asked everyone in turn what breed of dog they picked and why. Additionally, we discussed the contrasts between the dogs they picked as their two favorites and the dog they liked least.

Andrew began by explaining that he picked a Chihuahua for the dog he liked least.

Andrew: "They're so nervous. They're always anxious and shaking, not trusting. I feel like you try to reach out to them, and they don't trust you. They like to bite, and I don't like that. They're so fragile. It's like they're always afraid, saying 'Don't hurt me,' like a real scaredy cat."

GSS: "Your description sounds very different from the Collie and St. Bernard you described as very mellow and relaxed."

Andrew: "That's right. They're such anxious, little dogs. Usually you can't go to them and play with them, unless it's a puppy. Otherwise, they have this sense of 'Look at me, but don't touch me. I might bite you.' And I don't like that.

And I don't like people who are nervous and high strung either.

Additionally, Andrew had a second dog he didn't like – a Bulldog, though generally, people only select one Underdog and Andrew explained:

"I don't like Bulldogs, because they're ugly and they're mean. They look at you and want to growl all the time. Look at them too long, and they get defensive, such as with my neighbor's Bulldog. Look at him for a few seconds, and he starts growling. And some people think when you're looking at them, you're judging them, so they snap at you. They have this attitude of don't bother me, don't get in my face. And I don't like being around people like that, so that fits with my choosing a Bulldog as one of the dogs I least like."

Next, Flo, who previously chose a Golden Retriever and a German Shepherd as her two favorite dogs, described the Bloodhound as the dog she liked the least. The key reason was because she perceived the Bloodhound as a hard dog to control. As she commented:

"I don't like Bloodhounds because they're always chasing stuff and barking. There's a Bloodhound down the street who chases anything he sees – cats, chickens, buses, pigs. So his owner has to keep him locked up, and as soon as he gets out, he's out chasing things again – so I find Bloodhounds uncontrollable because they just chase everything. And they won't mind. They just take off on the chase."

GSS: "How about people that are like that?

Flo: "Yeah. There are some people you don't want to be bothered with, because they do what they want and don't listen to what you say. They don't care about cooperating with others. They either do what they want or want to be in charge, and I just want such people to leave me alone."

Then, Susan shared her Underdog choice, the English and Irish Setter because they didn't fit with her lifestyle. She liked staying close to home and participating in activities that didn't involve a lot of physical exercise or exertion, so she chose a pair of dogs who were very active as her Underdog. As she commented:

"With an English or Irish Setter, you have to be very active. You have to like physical activity, but that's not me. So I don't like outdoors animals. They want to go outside on walks, and if you like to run, that could be the dog for you. But for me, I don't want to be walking any miles trying to keep up with these dogs."

Heddy indicated that she didn't like the Chihuahua much like Andrew, because of its nervous, anxious nature. Plus she saw it as a dog that tended to withdraw from people, which didn't fit her style as a people person. As she noted:

"You can't get close to a Chihuahua. Like one day, I went to visit a friend who had one, and she had to chase him away from the door, because he blocked my way. He was just sitting there yapping, not wanting me to pass by, because he didn't want me to sit in a certain place. Then, I tried to pet him, but he began shaking, and each time I bent down to pet him, he went running to my friend. So I really can't stand this dog. He didn't want anybody to touch him or talk to him. He didn't want anybody to be there. So I didn't like him."

GGS: "Are there any people the Chihuahua reminds you of that you don't like?"

Heddy: Yeah. There are some people I know who are sneaky and some people from the neighborhood who come to my house bothering me. They don't say much, but just hang around, maybe smoking and drinking. They ask you if you mind, but if you tell them no, they ignore you."

Then, Susan, who had chosen the English or Irish Setter for her Underdog, based on not liking an active lifestyle, chimed in with reasons she didn't like the Chihuahua either. "It has a defensive, "small person's personality," which is characteristic of some people she didn't like a lot.

"The Chihuahua's personality is like a Napoleon or short-man's complex. They always try to take advantage of you by playing the victim role."

Then, the discussion turned to the way that dogs take on their owner's characteristics, whether or not the person picked that dog in the first place. As Susan pointed out:

"Sometimes you don't pick a dog, but then you bond with it and it'll take on your characteristics. That's what's amazing: your dog learns you. For example, I've always worked during the day, so Snowy (her Arctic German Shepherd) learned to sleep during the day. And now that I don't work during the day, she still keeps her same routine. She lies on her bed and goes to sleep. So once you train a dog, that's how they will react.

"And dogs pick up a lot of your personality, too. They can really sense what you are feeling and how you are relating to another person. For example, I can have a close friend over, and my dog is really cool with that. But, if we start to have an argument and the person starts to get too ugly, Snowy will come and stand by my side, like she's backing me up, and that'll make the other person back down or go."

Finally, Susan wondered what happens when people end up owning a dog they don't like –a dog they might choose as their Underdog? As Susan put it:

"Suppose dogs get with a person who has the wrong characteristics and personality? Would they change to be more like that person?"

I explained that such an outcome might not be the result. The relationship might be more like a dysfunctional union between people who don't fit well together. As I commented:

"If a dog and person don't make a good personality match, they might have trouble bonding, say when someone gets a dog that is unlike them. If you get a dog that's very outdoorsy, the dog will get very frustrated, because you're not going to take it out. Or say you get a Siberian Husky, which is a very independent, active dog. If you open the door, he'll run away.

"That's why it's important to choose a dog which makes a good fit with your own personality, and that's why there are all these personality tests to help people choose the kind of dog that feels right for them, and their lifestyle."

Finally, concluding the workshop, I explained how people might use the information they obtained about their two favorite and least favorite dogs to apply that in their personal life or in the workplace. For example, they might get insights on how to deal with problems with a boss, say to be stronger to keep a boss from taking advantage or holding back to avoid a confrontation.

Or they might use their Inner Dogs like spiritual helpers or teachers by imagining talking to them to get advice.

So, on that note, the workshop ended.

I have described this workshop at length to illustrate how you might work with your dogs by using a small group of friends or associates.

When you set up a workshop, keep in mind these general tips:

- Find a relaxed, comfortable, quiet place for the workshop.
- Choose a leader who has already selected his or her Top Dog, Watch Dog, and Underdog to lead the guided fantasy meditations, or prerecord the guided instructions on tape, speaking in a slow, quiet voice and leave a minute or two on the tapes for quiet reflection where indicated in the script. Still another possibility is for everyone to quietly reflect on the Dog Profiles and choose a Top Dog, Watch Dog, and Underdog that way.

- After participants select their Top Dog and Watch Dog, start a discussion in which each person describes the characteristics they associate with that dog (which may be those in the Dog Profiles or other qualities) and why they like or identify with that dog the most. Then, ask them to discuss how these characteristics describe themselves. Invite people to share stories about how they have expressed these qualities in different situations – and if people own dogs, invite them to talk about the traits they share with their dogs.
- After participants select their Underdog, have a discussion in which each person describes the characteristics they associate with that dog (which may be those in the Dog Profiles or other qualities) and why they don't like or least identify with that dog. Then, ask them to describe how they don't have these qualities or might want to get rid of them, and invite them to talk about any people with these characteristics they don't like. Invite people to share stories about how they have expressed these qualities in different situations.
- As much as possible, ask people to share in turn, although if people want to comment on what someone else has said or ask questions, invite them to do so.
- Keep the conversation focused on how the people have expressed the qualities of their chosen dogs. If the dog owners start to talk about experiences with their own dog or give tips on raising, caring for, and training dogs, gently guide the discussion back to focus on the traits of their favorite and least favorite dogs and how these traits are reflected in themselves and other people.
- Finally, have fun. Keep the mood fun and lighthearted, and feel free to do things to add to the mood (such as play the What Kind of Dog Are You song, make colored masks of dogs, have people draw pictures of their favorite and least favorite dogs. The idea is to both learn about yourself and others through this system, and have fun doing it.

CHAPTER 3: WORKING WITH YOUR DOG

Now that you know your Top Dog, Watch Dog, and Underdog, you can work with them to learn more about yourself and others. Then, use these insights to develop the characteristics you want, eliminate those you don't want, and work toward achieving your personal and professional goals. Use these techniques on your own, with a partner, or in a small group.

Consider them like your dog family, as long as they remain in these three positions, though as you change, you may welcome other dogs to your family.

If any are on your dog team of Guide Dogs or Power Dogs, you can call on them for that kind of help, too.

Learning More about Your Dog Family – and You!

A first step to working with your dog family is to learn more about them – and by extension, yourself. Work with your Top Dog and Watch Dog first; then meet your Underdog.

Getting to Know Your Top Dog and Watch Dog

Consider your Top Dog and Watch Dog as representing the qualities you have or would like to develop. Your Top Dog represents qualities that are strongest in you or that you most strongly want to acquire; your Watch Dog has those qualities, but not as strongly. This is like having a superior and inferior function or primary and secondary traits in the Myers-Briggs personality type system; or like having your birth sign and a rising sign in Astrology. Look at both aspects of yourself to promote a more rounded picture of you.

If you have chosen the same breed as your Top Dog and Watch Dog, that's like having the same birth sign and rising sign, like being a double Gemini or double Capricorn. You simply have those qualities or would like to develop them more strongly, though when you start the exercise for finding your Top Dog and Watch Dog, you may find a different Watch Dog.

Now, let's go. First move through this process with your Top Dog; then do the same with your Watch Dog.

Look at the Dog Profile corresponding to your Top Dog (and later your Watch Dog) and review the traits characterizing this type of dog. If you have other associations with this breed, add them. Get in a relaxed frame of mind and reflect on these different traits.

As you look at these traits, make a list in any order of all the traits you feel you have or want to acquire. You can use the chart on the following page to help you do this. For each trait, put down the number 1, 2, or 3, depending on how strongly you feel you have that trait or would like to acquire it. The higher the number, the more strongly you feel about that trait.

Do this yourself for both your Top Dog and Watch Dog, unless they're the same; then just do this once. This process will help you think about the qualities you have and those you want to develop. Later you will use this information in other exercises to gain more insight into yourself and how you see yourself in the future.

Traits of my Top Dog:
Type of Dog:_____

Traits	Traits I Have (use 1-3 to indicate their strength)	Traits I'd Like to Acquire or Further Develop (use 1-3 to indicate their strength)

Traits of my Watch Dog:

Type of Dog:_____

Traits	Traits I Have (use 1-3 to indicate their strength)	Traits I'd Like to Acquire or Further Develop (use 1-3 to indicate their strength)

Putting Yourself in the Picture

Now that you have consciously thought about how your Top Dog and Watch Dog represent your current traits and how you want to be in the future, reflect on this information using your intuition. To do so, get very relaxed and use any or all of the following exercises to gain more insight. The first is a reflective exercise in which you ask yourself questions; the next is a visualization in which you see yourself becoming one with your dog, so you feel the connection more closely; the third is a physical exercise.

1) Picture This!

Hold the profile sheet with the picture of your dog and the description of characteristic personality traits in front of you. Then, in a very relaxed, reflective state, ask yourself a series of questions. Don't try to guide the answers; just let them come to you, as self-talk in your mind, or imagine that your chosen dog is answering you. As the answers come to you, write them down or say them into a recorder, so you can remember and review them later.

Start with the following questions, and add any additional questions that deal with issues important to you.
- In what ways does this dog reflect me?
- What common personality traits or characteristics do we share?
- What traits stand out as especially characteristic of us?
- What kind of traits does this dog have that I would like to have or develop further?
- What kind of changes might I make in myself to develop these traits I would like to have or further develop?
- How can this dog help me make these changes?
- How would or does this dog fit into my current lifestyle?
- In what ways might I change my current lifestyle to better suit this dog?
- What do I need to do now to make these changes?
- How can this dog help me make these changes?

- What else does this dog have to tell me about who I would like to be?
- What other questions might I ask at this time? (Then listen to the questions that come to mind and ask them).

2) **Putting on the Dog Head**

In this technique, you seek to feel a closer connection with your chosen dog by imagining that you and your dog have become one. It's a technique you can use to connect better with people, too, so you can see the world from their point of view by walking in their shoes. Using this metaphor, you might imagine yourself walking with their dog paws to see the world and yourself in a whole new way.

To start the process, you can read the following visualization as a guide and then do it. Or read this into a recorder and play it back as you listen and visualize.

To begin, gaze at the picture of the dog you have chosen – or if you own a real dog of this type, gaze at that. Look deep into the dog's eyes, and imagine that you both are becoming one. Imagine that you are coming closer and closer to each other. Finally, you merge, and as you do, see yourself placing the dog's head on your own; see your own arms and legs become the feet and paws of the dog.

Then, feeling this sense of oneness or this sense that you have become this dog, look around the world as this dog. First look around your house. Since you now have a better sense of hearing and smell, pay more attention to what you hear and notice any smells around you.

Then, imagine you are going outside your house as this dog. In your mind's eye, go out your door and pay attention to what you see, hear, smell, or feel. Notice the path or soft dirt beneath your feet. Walk or run across the grass. Notice if there are people in the lawn or on the street, and trot by, weaving in and out of any people there. If someone reaches down to pet you, enjoy the sensation on your back and keep on going.

Should you see any cars, stop and let them pass by, and keep going. You feel curious, interested in exploring and observing what's out there, and you know you can always quickly run back home.

So take a few minutes, now experiencing the world around you as the dog you have chosen. If you meet any people or dogs along the way, know that they will be very friendly and helpful. And some will be very curious. They want to know a little about who you are. So if they ask, be ready to tell them. Tell them who you are and how you have gone out to explore. So just look around and see what you discover. You'll find you are drawn to things you are most interested in – such as people walking along, objects on the street, playground equipment with tunnels to crawl through, or other dogs.

Now as you move on, you come to a shiny mirror lying on the grass or on the side of the road. Go over to that mirror and look into it. You'll see your own face or your dog's face peering back at you – or maybe a combination of your two faces. As you look in this mirror, you can ask a series of questions about yourself. Start with these few questions and listen for the answers. Don't try to guide the answers. Just let them come to you. Then, you can add in additional questions and listen for those answers or you may see them appear in the mirror.

Here are a few first questions to ask; then add your own:
- Who am I? How would I describe myself, if someone asked me this question?
- What are my strongest traits? My weakest?
- Is there anything about me I'd like to change? And how?
- Is there anything I should do differently?
- What should I do now?

Now, ask your own questions. What else do you want to know about yourself?

When the questions and answers stop coming, turn away from the mirror and walk back the way you came through the grass or on the road. As you return to where you started, count slowly from 1 to 5, becoming more and conscious as you do…1….2….3….more and more awake….4…and 5 – you're back in the room.

Once you're back, take a few minutes to write down what you have learned on a sheet of paper or in your notebook, so you can remember and review this information later and put it into practice in your everyday life.

3) <u>Dancing Your Dog</u>

Another method to feel closer to your dog traces back to the dawn of human history – the technique of dancing an animal to feel a closer connection with it and draw on that quality for oneself. Sometimes the dancers put on masks representing the animal they are dancing, to feel the bond more firmly. The difference here is that you are going to "dance your dog".

This technique is also a fun way to experiment with what it's like to act like a dog –like putting on a mask and dog costume for Halloween or to go to a costume party.

Before dancing, you can create images of your dog to add to the sense of personal transformation into something else. For example, create a mask to put on or put a picture of your dog on your jacket and wear that. Or put a poster or statue of your dog on a table or counter, to focus on it as you dance. Or use a combination of any of these possibilities. You goal is to strengthen the sense of transformation through the physical experience with visual, auditory and other cues, so you are more completely immersed in the experience. You might even include the sounds of dogs barking in the background for additional realism.

To prepare for the experience, put on a rhythmic recording to listen to. Or use drums, rattles, or other instruments to make sounds and provide a recurring beat to help you feel the experience more intensely. (Or if you are working with a partner or in a group, you can take turns having one or two people play, while the others dance.)

Once you are ready, start the music, and let yourself go for 10-15 minutes, longer if you want to keep going. Just feel the sounds going through you, and as you do, imagine you are becoming one with your dog. Imagine the dog's head on yours, and you are dancing as this dog. For now, don't ask any questions. Just let yourself go, so you fully feel the sense of transformation. As you do, move as you imagine your dog walks. React to others who pass by as your dog might. Notice any sounds in the room besides the music. Become aware of any smells. And feel free to bark, howl, or otherwise make the sounds your dog might make.

When the music ends or you feel ready to stop, turn off the music, and quietly stand or sit (or get down on all fours) so you feel the sense of being your dog.

Then, holding onto that feeling, ask yourself the questions listed in the previous exercise. These are:
- *Who am I? How would I describe myself, if someone asked me this question?*
- *What are my strongest traits? My weakest?*
- *Is there anything about me I'd like to change? And how?*
- *Is there anything I should do differently?*
- *What should I do now?*

Add your own questions to ask what else you want to know about yourself.

Keep going until you feel you are running out of questions and answers. Then, write down what you have experienced, so you can remember and refer to this later.

Watching Out with Your Watch Dog

After you explore ways to better understand yourself and what to change or develop with your Top Dog, go through the same process with your Watch Dog. Then, take some time to compare and reflect on the different results.

Your insights from working with your Top Dog indicate your strengths or what you most want to develop, while the insights from your Watch Dog indicate additional areas of strength and development.

If you get the same insights from both, that's a double message underlining your strength in this area or emphasizing that this is an area to focus on developing.

If you get different insights, regard those as additional traits or strengths that you have or additional qualities to work on developing, to become even more well-rounded. Generally, focus on developing the qualities represented by your Top Dog first.

Celebrating Your Strengths

Once you have identified your top qualities and strengths, it's time to celebrate and affirm them to yourself. The next chapter will deal will making changes on the traits or qualities to develop. But first, focus on the great traits and strengths that make up you – the qualities you share with your Top Dog and Watch Dog.

So go back to the lists you have already made–The Traits of My Top Dog and The Traits of My Watch Dog – and create a list with your strongest traits first, then your next strongest, and finally your least strongest (which also may be traits you want to further develop). You can use "My Qualities and Strengths" chart page to do this.

Then, create a fun environment to celebrate yourself. For example, go to your favorite room in the house, put on some bouncy music, put out a small cake or plate of cookies with a candle. Perhaps hang up pictures of the breed of dogs you have chosen as your Top Dog and Watch Dog. Do whatever you want to create a festive setting. Plus include a glass of wine or juice to toast yourself. If you want, add some small blue ribbons or buttons to symbolize the awards you are giving to yourself – much like a judge at a dog show might give an award to an owner and their dog. Now, this is your award to you to remind yourself what a winner you are.

Then, as you look at the list, imagine your Top Dog and Watch Dog are with you in spirit, perhaps even sitting on either side of you, and think or say the following "I am great because…" affirmations. Fill in each of the traits you have listed as you do this. After you state each affirmation, pick up your glass of wine or juice and drink a toast to yourself. You might also pat yourself on the back, take a bow, or applaud to compliment yourself. Finally, if you have some ribbons or buttons, give one to yourself, as your "Blue Ribbon" award for being you and having the great qualities you do.

Following are some of the affirmations you might use. Just fill in the traits you have on the list:

"I am great because I am_____"
"I'm wonderful because I_____"
"People really like me because I_____"

After you finish celebrating each of these traits, give yourself a final round of applause, take a final bow, give yourself a large blue ribbon, and/or drink a final toast to yourself to recognize the many ways in which you are great. Then, say a final thank you to your Top Dog and Watch Dog for helping you recognize these qualities in yourself, and take a minute or two to savor how great you feel for honoring and celebrating yourself.

My Top Qualities and Strengths	
My Strongest Traits:	
My Next Strongest Traits:	
My Least Strongest Traits:	

Making Your Top Dog and Watch Dog Part of Your Everyday Life

Beyond getting insights from your Top Dog and Watch Dog, you can make an even closer connection with them and remind yourself about how great you are and how you are further developing yourself every day in two ways – you can find representations of your Top Dog and Watch Dog and post visible reminders to yourself.

Here are some things you can do:
- Find a small furry stuffed dog or ceramic statue of the same breed as your Top Dog and/or Watch Dog and put it in a prominent place in your house. Besides using stuffed dogs or statues for a decorative reminder, you can use it during exercises as a focus to represent your Top Dog or Watch Dog.
- Put up a poster featuring the same breed as your Top Dog and/or Watch Dog.
- Get greeting cards or postcards featuring the same breed as your Top Dog and/or Watch Dog.
- Put up "My Top Qualities and Strengths" list in a place where you will see it each day, such as in the bathroom, on your bedroom door, or on the side of the refrigerator.
- Get a small keychain-sized image of the breed of your Top Dog and/or Watch Dog and dangle it from your car mirror.
- Make a rubber stamp with the image of the breed of your Top Dog and/or Watch Dog, and use it on your letters.
- Put pictures of the breed of your Top Dog and/or Watch Dog on your Website or on your Weblog if you have one.

Additionally, you might imagine that your Top Dog and Watch Dog are accompanying you and lending their support as you go about your daily activities, along with any Guide Dogs or Power Dogs you are calling on for help. The process is much like what is done in many traditions, where people call on a spiritual guide, inner teacher, or helper. Now, you can call on your Top Dog and Watch Dog, too, as well as your Guide Dogs and Power Dogs.

How the Process Works

How well does this process work? Here are some examples of people gaining insights from the dogs they preferred or identified with in one of my workshops.

Nancy picked a Bassett Hound as her first choice and owns one. She felt a close identification with her choice and found they shared many of the same personality traits. And sometimes her dog's behavior served as a reminder to her of how to behave.

Why choose a Basset Hound? Because she felt drawn to it as a nurse and very warm person. She thought the Bassett Hound's similar warm, affectionate qualities made it a perfect companion to take to a senior center where she volunteered. As Nancy explained: "My dog Marci loves being with the elderly people. Marci's so gentle and loving, and she has the same care and compassion for others that I have. Also, she's got the same concern with behaving and doing what's right."

Nancy gave an example. "Sometimes I correct her, just like my mother used to correct me when I was a kid. I remember one time Marci got really excited when the mailman came, and she barked really ferociously – very unusual for her, because she is usually so calm and placid. But I quickly looked her in the eye and said "No", and she looked taken aback and guilty. She hung her head sheepishly and retreated to the living room. After that, when the mailman came, I saw her looking at me, as if to say, 'I know I shouldn't do that.' Then, she ran into the living room and didn't bark. Her behavior reminded me very much of me. I like to do what's right, and I very much like the approval that comes from knowing I've done the right thing."

By the same token, whether you own the dog or not, you might imagine your Top Dog or Watch Dog sitting beside you or walking with you giving you insights about yourself.

To take another example, in another workshop, one woman encountered a tiger and a panther who she thought represented two aspects of herself; an experience much like working with one's Top Dog and Watch Dog. As she thought about the qualities of the tiger and panther, she saw how they expressed her own qualities and suggested what she needed to do to develop herself – by seeking more balance in her life while she was going through a period of making choices.

Here's how she reported her experience and came to her insights, with the help of these two animals:

"When the journey started out, I came into a jungle, and the first animal that I met was a monkey, and he jumped on me. But I knew it wasn't my power animal. It was more like he was a greeter, just showing me the way.

Then I met a tiger and a black panther and they had very different qualities. The tiger reminded me of the tiger I had dreamt about twice the last two weeks. In both dreams, I slept with the tiger, and the tiger was very loving. We slept in each other's arms, like old friends. As for the panther, he reminded me of my sun sign, which is Scorpio. It's a very sharp, penetrating sign which represents my very deep, cutting edge that's harsh and slices through things.

So it felt like the tiger and the panther were my two sides. I felt like the tiger was the soft part, the panther the hard part, and now I felt drawn to that soft part. So instead of walking along with the tiger, I decided to go inside it, and it felt very good and powerful being in there.

Then, I switched back and forth, walking between those two cats and being inside the tiger. It was like I was experiencing the polarity of yin and yang, and finding that balance between them.

When I went inside the tiger, I felt very grounded. I felt a wonderful, strong, powerful feeling of being inside and being the cat, and I felt this wonderful feeling of soft power, which was helping me come to term with my female power by experiencing this warmth and nurturing, which I need right now. So it's like this tiger was my soft feminine aspect, while the panther was my cutting and aggressive masculine side.

I felt like having both of them walking side by side with me was showing me the two aspects of my power, which I'm trying to come to terms with, by getting more in touch with my feminine side."

As these examples illustrate, the process of finding your Top Dog or Watch Dog can be a powerful way of gaining personal insights, whether you own the dog or not, much like the taking a journey to connect with any animal representing you can provide deep insights about yourself and what to do next for your personal and professional development. Then you can later further your journey to learn even more.

Getting to Know Your Underdog

Now it's finally time to get to know your Underdog, that represents the qualities you don't have or least like in yourself and want to eliminate. You may not naturally want to look at these Underdog qualities but a key part of personal and professional development is getting rid of any traits you least like and replacing them with those you want.

You'll use the same kind of exercises as you used to better get to know your Top Dog and Watch Dog, but now your focus will be on getting rid of qualities, rather than embracing them.

First, pull out the Dog Profile corresponding to your Underdog. Now, look at this description and review the traits characterizing this type of dog. If you have other associations with this breed, add them. Then, in a relaxed frame of mind, reflect on these different traits and particularly on those you don't like.

Now, as you look at these traits, make a list of all the traits or characteristics you don't like about this dog, which is why this dog is your Underdog. Note any traits which you feel you now have but don't like about yourself; these are the traits you want to get rid of.

You can use the chart on the following page to help you make your list. List all the traits that come to mind in no particular order. Then, for each trait, put down the number 0, 1, 2, or 3, depending on how strongly you feel you have that trait. If you have put down a "0", great; time to celebrate because you don't have that trait. Then, in the next column, indicate how strongly you would like to get rid of those traits you don't like. (The higher the number, the more strongly you feel).

This process will help you think about the qualities you have and don't want in yourself.

Traits of my Underdog:

Type of Dog:_____

Traits	Traits I Have (use 0-3 to indicate their strength)	Traits I'd Like to Get Rid of (use 1-3 to indicate strength)

1) What's Wrong with This Picture?

Start by holding the profile sheet with the picture of your dog in front of you. Then, in a relaxed, reflective state, ask yourself a series of questions. Don't try to guide the answers, just let them come to you, either as self-talk in your mind, or imagine that the dog you have chosen is answering you. As the answers come to you, write them down or say them into a recorder to remember and review them later.

Start with the following questions. Add additional questions that deal with issues important to you.
- Why do I least like this particular dog?
- What traits does it have that I don't like?
- Which of these traits that I don't like do I also have?
- What traits would I like to get rid of in myself?
- What kind of changes might I make in myself to get rid of these traits? How can this dog help me make these changes?
- What else does this dog have to tell me about who I am or would like to be?
- What other questions might I ask at this time? (Listen to the questions that come to mind and ask them).

2) Putting Out the Dog

In this technique, you seek to experience an even stronger feeling of getting rid of those traits you don't want by imagining that you are putting out the dog. You can use this technique to mentally eliminate negative or difficult people from your life, too. See yourself opening the door and sending the dog away –to a backyard doghouse or further away than that.

As an alternative to doing this as a visualization, ask yourself: "What are the reasons I don't like this dog?" Then, think of any reasons that first pop into your mind and write them down. Review that list and notice what qualities you have yourself which you don't like. Choose one or two to focus on as qualities to work on eliminating from your life – and skip to the next section.

To start the visualization process, you can read the following guide and then do it. Or read this into a recorder and play it back as you listen and visualize.

> *To begin, gaze at the picture of the dog you have chosen. Look deep into its eyes, and as you do, think about the reasons that you don't like this dog. Notice the qualities that you don't like in this dog and that you don't want in yourself. Focus on the one or two qualities you most dislike and most want out of your life.*
>
> *Then, in your mind's eye, imagine that this dog is in your house. It might be in the kitchen begging for food; in the living room making noise; in the bedroom making a mess. Wherever it is, you don't want it there anymore, because it has those qualities you don't like in the dog and in yourself.*
>
> *Now call that dog to you, and if it doesn't want to come, since it may be badly behaved, snap on its leash and pull it to you. Then, lead your dog to your back door and open it.*
>
> *Now as you stand there, think about the reasons you want this dog out of your life. Think about the qualities it has that you don't want, to remind yourself why you are getting rid of this dog.*
>
> *Then, tell the dog to go out and go to its dog house – or just tell it to go. Explain why it has to go in various ways. You might say: "I don't want you anymore…It's time to go…You are not welcome here anymore."*
>
> *Even if the dog looks sad or doesn't want to go, keep repeating these words to reinforce your message. If your dog still sits waiting, hoping you'll let it back in, simply tap it on the back, push it out, and shut the door.*
>
> *As your Underdog leaves, watch it go, feeling that it is taking the trait or traits you don't want away with it.*

Later, you can use this experience as a reminder that you don't want this trait, that you are getting rid of it, that it is gone or going away.

Finally, as you see your Underdog disappear in the distance or go into its dog house, turn away from the door. Walk back into your living room, feeling very free and comfortable that your Underdog and the trait or traits you want to get rid of are gone and unlikely to reappear. Then, count slowly from 1 to 5, becoming more and conscious as you do…1….2….3….more and more awake….4…and 5 – you're back in present day reality.

Once you're back, take a few minutes to write down what you have experienced on a sheet of paper or in your notebook, and end with a positive affirmation about the trait or traits you have sent away with your dog. For example, note something like: "My anger is gone…I'm not angry anymore…I'll be calmer in the future." You might even put these comments on cards around your house as a reminder of the trait or traits you want out of your life.

3) Going, Going, Gone

To further emphasize that this quality you don't want is gone, physically sweep it away. Just like "Dancing the Dog" is an adaptation of the technique of dancing an animal that traces back to the dawn of human history this method is modeled after the technique of eliminating negative forces by sweeping them away. Such techniques have been traditionally used to get rid of illness or unfriendly spirits through various means – from brooms to brushes to bundles of leaves to cleanse a person. Here the technique is adapted to getting rid of qualities you don't want in yourself – like "making a clean sweep", where you sweep out the old, and open yourself up to the new.

You can visualize this process by imagining that you are using a broom, brush, or bundle of leaves – or better yet, hold a broom, brush, or leaf bundle in your hands, and physically do this cleansing and sweeping. Doing this physically makes this experience even more intense, so you feel this sense of ridding yourself of unwanted traits more clearly. You can use a broom or brush you find around the house, or create a bundle of leaves by gathering fallen leaves from your backyard or park, since these are already dead. To prepare for the experience, put on a rhythmic piece of music to listen to, particularly one with a strong forceful beat to underline your strength and power in taking action. Or use drums, rattles, or other instruments to make sounds and provide a recurring beat to feel the experience more intensely. If you are working with a partner or group, you can take turns having one or two people play, while the others dance.

    Once you are ready, start the music, and let yourself go for 5-10 minutes, longer if you want to keep going. Just feel the sounds going through you and imagine that your Underdog is in a circle with you. Then, in your imagination – or in reality if you are holding a real broom, brush, or bundle of leaves – begin sweeping or brushing the trait or traits you don't want away. As you do, your Underdog backs off, moving further and further away, as you sweep or brush harder and harder. As it moves back, imagine that it is taking the trait or traits you don't want in yourself with it. So more and more you are casting off these qualities.

    Finally, your Underdog turns and runs out of the room. As it does, imagine that these qualities are going away, too. Finally, when you can no longer see your Underdog, imagine these traits are gone for good and even say those words aloud to yourself. "They are gone…gone…gone."

    When the music ends or you feel ready to stop, turn it off, and quietly stand or sit (or get down on all fours), so you feel the sense of satisfaction at sending away that trait or traits. So you feel a sense of cleansing and of being newly liberated and free.

Moving On

    The exercises in this chapter have provided different ways for learning more about your chosen dogs and yourself. By knowing who you are and want to be, you can think about what to do to get there. Then with these insights, you can work with your Top Dog, Watch Dog, and Underdog to help you make these changes – or call on your Guide Dogs and Power Dogs, as well, so you have your whole Dog Team behind you, helping you change.

CHAPTER 4: FIND YOUR INNER GUIDE DOG – OR DOGS

Even before choosing your favorite dog or the one most like you, you can get help from your inner guide dog or a team of dogs that sometimes may be the same as your Top Dog or Watch Dog or could later attain this position.

Essentially, an inner guide dog is one you can call on for assistance in various circumstances – from setting goals to dealing with difficult situations. The process works much like calling on any inner help for guidance, strength, wisdom, and power with the assistance of a spiritual guide, helper, teacher, angel, or animal guide. It's an approach used in many traditions – from traditional religions to spiritual paths to New Age groups.

Now you can call on one of the many breeds of dogs for help. Just call on the guide that seems most suitable for you in a particular situation. It could be one you turn to regularly – or call on a different dog for different occasions, or as a comic might say, you simply turn to your "inner guide dog" by calling up images of that dog in your mind's eye. Then, you ask that dog to help in various ways.

Here's how the process works.

Which Guide Dog Is for You?

The great thing in calling on your inner guide dog is you can look for different dogs to help you in different situations. They can be dogs you are already familiar with, or use the Dog Profiles to become acquainted with other breeds and types of dogs.

You are simply calling on a type of dog that can give you the most help under the circumstances. Say you are struggling to lose weight and so far no diet has helped, and you just don't have the will-power to stay on it. That's where your guide dog comes in.

You pick a dog that might be especially good to help you strengthen your resolve, such as a Standard Poodle or Afghan Hound, who both are known for being thin, beautiful, and stylish.

Then, with the image of that dog in mind, call on it to give you advice and remind you to stay on target. You might also take steps to remind yourself to call on that dog, such putting up a poster with its picture on the bathroom wall, where you will see it several times a day. Or make or buy a sculpture of that dog.

Some people have regular conversations with their guide dogs, too. The process works much like self-talk, where you have a dialogue with yourself – or a group discussion between different parts of you. But instead, you talk to your inner guide dog like a helpful friend, advisor, or teacher, just like any spiritual guide or helper. Contacting your Guide Dog is a way of personifying a part of you. What makes this process especially helpful is turning an abstract voice in your head into a "real" being, so you gain more support, as you might from a real person offering to help.

Using Your Inner Guide Dog for Different Purposes

While some people may like calling on the same dog for different purposes, others may prefer finding dogs with different qualities to help them with issues that call for those qualities.

Take Mary, an administrative assistant, who has found it comfortable to call on a Collie to help in different situations. She was especially drawn to a Collie after doing an exercise to look for her Guide Dog, and she found calling in the dogs helped her feel more comfortable in a high-conflict work environment. When she heard some co-workers arguing down the hall and felt herself getting tense, she would lean back and call on the image of this warm, protective Collie to appear and tell her to relax. And, she would. Or if her critical boss berated her for something, she would imagine the Collie by her side, telling her: "Be cool. Be cool." So she was able to keep her cool – and her job, rather than telling off the boss in the heat of the moment.

Subsequently, she called on the Collie to help with other tasks, reasoning that if he helped her in these circumstances, he would be a worthy helper in other situations. Then, as she thought this, the Collie would give her the help she needed because you give the dogs you call on the power to help by calling them into reality.

But often, people call on different breeds of dogs in different situations, based on the qualities they associate with that dog. For example, if you feel too tense much of the time and want to become more relaxed, maybe call on the Beagle or Bassett Hound, because these are two very laid-back dogs. They are often found parked on the family couch or cozy armchair, and like to hang out. By calling up the image of either dog, you similarly cause yourself to become more relaxed.

Or suppose you want more "Power", because you were left behind at work after a round of promotions. You think you aren't being recognized for your true worth, because you don't have enough power and you feel a need to be more assertive, aggressive, and thick-skinned to get the recognition from others to get ahead. In this case, a likely candidate for your inner guide dog might be the Great Dane, Mastiff, or Bull Mastiff. These are strong, powerful, big dogs – and an infusion of this image might be just what you need to help you take on your co-workers and boss. For instance, as you focus on that image at home, you can see the power you want pouring into you. Then, you can go to work with that sense of the Great Dane or Mastiff within you.

Some Exercises to Connect and Communicate with Your Inner Guide Dog

If you are already familiar with different breeds of dogs, start with the exercises right away. If not, take some time to review the Dog Type Profiles or list of dogs to become familiar with them and feel you really know them.

Then, you can use various exercises to connect with your Inner Guide Dog just to get acquainted or for help with a particular issue. Use the exercises that feel most comfortable for you.

As an alternative to doing a visualization, ask yourself the question: "Which dog would I like to be my Guide Dog?" and listen to the first impression or thought that comes to mind. Then, repeat the question to pick additional Guide Dogs. While these visualization exercises are fun and help you access your intuition and powers of creativity, you can tap into your these abilities in other ways.

To do any of the visualization exercises, first get into a comfortable, relaxed state. To help you relax, you can use repetitive drumming, listen to relaxing soothing music, or focus on your breathing as you count backward slowly from10 to 1. Then, use one of the following exercises. Use the descriptions below as a general guide or recite the exercises into a recorder, play it back, relax, and enjoy your journey to meet your dog.

Before you begin, decide if you want to connect with a Dog Guide generally or for help with a particular issue or problem. In the latter case, keep that issue or problem in mind as you go on your journey.

Pet Store

In the following guided journey, you'll imagine going to a pet store where you see many different kinds of dogs and choose one.

Now imagine that you are going into a very large pet store either to find a dog guide to help you generally or to help with a particular problem or issue. You arrive in the parking lot, park, and walk into the store.

As you walk in, you see a large ring where many dogs are exercising. Then you see several long rows with dogs of different breeds sitting in small cubicles or cages.

As you walk along through the rooms, some of the dogs move forward to greet you. Nod or smile at them as you pass. You may find that one dog is particularly eager to greet you, or you feel particularly drawn to that dog.

Stop and take some time to make a connection with that dog. You can shake its paw, perhaps imagine that you have become that dog's owner. Then, talk to it. Ask it some questions about what it likes and doesn't, what activities it prefers, and most importantly how it can help you. Don't try to control the answers to your questions; just let them come to you.

If you feel comfortable with that dog and would like it to become your helper, take it home with you. Lead it out or pick it up and take it to your car.

Then, with the dog on the seat beside or behind you, drive home slowly, feeling very confident and secure that you have found your Inner Dog guide to help you generally or with a particular problem.

Dog Director

In this case, you imagine yourself as a director of a movie which deals with the area where you want help. Start by consciously deciding on the issues you want help with – or if you're not sure, let that come to you. The following guided journey will help you become this director and find your "cast" of "top dogs" to help you with this "movie".

Imagine that you are a director for a movie that deals with an issue where you need help in your life. If you haven't already decided what the movie will be about, decide now. Think about what problems or concerns are most important to you and see that scene in your life playing out on the movie screen in your mind. Notice what particularly bothers you, what is especially difficult, and where you would like some help.

Now imagine that you are putting out a casting call for help. After you do, you see a number of dogs come in through the door and head over to a bench by the wall. They sit down side by side in a long row.

Now you go over to talk to them one by one, or you call them in turn to come over to you. Conduct your interview to ask each dog how he or she can help. Look for ways a particular dog might be likely to help. For example, say you are having a problem being assertive and powerful; maybe a large powerful dog would be especially helpful. Or suppose the issue involves relationships and teamwork. Maybe a dog that is especially friendly and good with people would help. Don't try to direct the answers; just let them come to you.

Should other dogs suddenly appear for an interview, that's fine. Just invite them in. Or if you feel you would like more dogs to talk to, imagine you are extending your casting call.

Now take some time to talk to each of the dogs. As you do, ask questions, such as: "How can you help me?" "What would you do in this situation?" or "What would you like to see happen in this film?"

Then, invite the dog or dogs you feel would be most helpful to join you on the set. As you see the movie play out before you, ask that dog to help you direct the outcome. You can either ask for advice or invite the dog to go into the movie. For instance, say you want to stand up to someone; that dog might go in front of that person and bark. Say you want a warmer relationship with someone. You might imagine the dog bounding on the set to be affectionate with that person.

Now, take some time to ask your guide dog (or dogs) for help and let them give you that help.

Finally, when you feel ready to wrap up your movie for the day, thank your guide dog (or dogs) for the help you have received, knowing you can always call on that dog for guidance and help in the future.

Dog Team Leader

Another technique for finding your Guide Dogs is viewing yourself as a "Dog Team Leader", assembling your team to help you get to a goal or resolve a problem. This time, instead of using a visualization, you'll create a list of major issues or areas to improve and the type of Dog Guide who might most help in that area.

These areas correspond to the 12 dimensions or "Dog Houses" on the Dog Star. You may find some of the same guides can help in different areas – or different dogs may be most helpful in each area.

Just go down the list and think of the first dog that comes to mind to help you with this area. Later, you can always go back and come up with other helpers to replace or add to those you have selected. It helps to develop an ongoing relationship with your guides over time, just as you might get more help by cultivating a continuing relationship with a friend, teacher, or counselor. Then, you can always seek-out extra help from other sources, or you can even bring in experts when you need more specialized help. So, why not with your Guide Dogs? They are there to help you – so seek out the guides who offer the most help under the current circumstances.

Digging Deep to Find Your Guide Dogs

In the following technique, you journey deep into the earth to meet your Guide Dogs. This technique draws on the shamanic journeying approach that has become increasingly popular as the subject of many workshops and seminars on "Shamanism" today, although it is an ancient tradition that goes back to the dawn of human society. You can use this technique to meet any power animals or teachers, although I adapted one of the exercises to focus on meeting your Guide Dogs.

So now, get your dog sled, so to speak, and be ready to travel on it to another world. Use the following guided journey as a general instruction by reading it beforehand, or read it into a recorder and play it back as you relax and take your journey.

Start by getting relaxed, and in a few minutes, you'll be going on a journey into the lower world. First, focus on your breathing to get in this relaxed state. Notice your breath going in and out, in and out. You find yourself getting relaxed, but you are also staying alert and awake. Let your breathing go in and out; in and out; feeling very peaceful and relaxed, yet very aware as well.

Be aware of your purpose in going on this journey below the earth. You are going to meet a power animal – in this case, one of your inner Guide Dogs. But don't try to meet that dog yet or decide what kind of dog you want to meet. Just let that happen when you go down there.

Find an opening to go down to this lower world. This opening could be someplace in the country, or city, someplace you're familiar with, or someplace new. It's some kind of opening going down to the ground.

See yourself going to the opening. As you go in, you find yourself in a tunnel or tube, and you feel very comfortable and very safe. There's plenty of room to move around. See or experience yourself moving through this tunnel. You are going down, down. Then, as you come to the bottom or end of this tunnel, it opens up into this lower world.

Now look around. Notice what you see, hear, feel. Notice your surroundings. It could be a little like a cave, or it could open up on a landscape. Experience yourself moving and looking around in this lower world, noticing what you see, feel. Experience whatever happens.

Now start going around to look for your Guide Dog. As you look, you may see different animals and different kinds of dogs wandering around. One of these dogs will stand out for you, come to you, or seem drawn to you. Or if you don't see that dog at once, keep going and pass by other places, other animals, until you feel drawn to one of these dogs or notice one that seems drawn to you. Then, go over to that dog or have it come to you.

Now meet it; get acquainted. Simply talk to it, and make friends with it. As you talk to or experience that dog, you may feel that this dog represents a little part of you, too. So, notice the qualities that dog has, and as you do, you might notice how these represent qualities of yourself.

You might also ask that dog if it has anything to tell you about itself, such as where it has been, what it does in the lower world, what it likes to do, or other questions. Then, listen to its response.

Now, as you get to know this dog, feel this dog is ready to be helpful. You can come back and visit this dog again and call on it for the help or advice you need in the future. The more you get to know this dog, the more help it will give you, and the more it will be a source of information and power for you.

If you want, follow this dog around and let it take you on a short journey, so you can explore a little bit more of this lower world and notice what's there. There's a path there you can follow. It could be straight or it might wander around. As you travel along it, you feel very safe taking this path, for your Guide Dog is with you. And you know this is just the beginning of exploring this world. Later, when you come back, you can meet this Guide Dog again, or you can meet other Guide Dogs and explore further. But for now, keep walking around with your Guide Dog. As you do, you might be aware of the heat, or coolness. You might be aware of the sounds around you. You might notice if there are any smells. Just get a real sense of this total environment as you explore.

Now, you are ready to go back. So you turn around, and your Guide Dog is starting to lead you back to where you first met it. On the way, your Guide Dog tells you that he will be there waiting for you the next time you come to see him. If you find this Guide Dog continues to be helpful, you can continue to visit it. But feel free to go back to meet other Guide Dogs, that can be helpful to you later.

Now you are back where you first met. So say good-bye to your Guide Dog as you would to any friend.

Then, travel back along the same path, and go back to the tunnel again. Now you are traveling through the tunnel back to the opening.

At the opening, step back out to where you began, and start counting backward from five to one. As you do, you will feel more and more awake and alert, and come back into the room. Five, four, more and more awake. Three, two, just about back. One, and you are back in the room.

Now that you have met your Guide Dog, as in other exercises to meet these dogs, think about what this experience means and how your Guide Dog can help you.

A Chart to Keep Track of Your Guide Dogs and How They Can Help

Use this chart to list your Guide Dogs. As you complete your list, feel free to repeat the breeds of dogs to call on for help. You can select more than one type of Guide Dog for each category, and later select one as your primary Guide Dog or work with those you have selected as a team. You can give each Guide Dog a name, or wait until you call on that dog for help.

LIST OF GUIDE DOGS		
Type of Issue	Breed of Guide Dog to be Asked for Help	Name of Helper
Becoming stronger and more powerful		
Exercising leadership		
Becoming more assertive		
Having more energy		
Working faster and smarter		
Achieving more balance in my activities and life		
Become a better people person		
Increasing my ability to influence others		
Becoming a better team player		
Improving my ability to think and remember		
Improving my style and appearance		
Developing selected personality traits		
Other:		
Other:		

Getting the Help You Need

However you have chosen your Guide Dogs, you can turn to them at any time – just as you might with any kind of inner guide or inner voice– from using spiritual helpers and teachers to self-talk.

Initially, it helps to use some quiet time to develop the relationship. By taking time to know each of your Guide Dogs as friends and companions, this will help you open up communication channels and feel comfortable turning to them, so later, they will be there when you want their help.

Getting Acquainted

To get acquainted, spend about 15-20 minutes a day having a mental dialogue with one or more of your Guide Dogs. A good way to do so is by getting relaxed in a quiet room in your house. An ideal time is just before you go to bed.

If you keep a journal, you can write down your conversations and thoughts there. Or use automatic writing to record the advice you get by writing in a very relaxed state, where you become a channel for whatever thoughts or words come to you. Then, you write them down without consciously thinking about what you are writing. In effect, your unconscious is speaking to you – through the communication you get from your Guide Dogs.

Asking for Help

When you are ready and receptive, start the conversation or dialogue as you might with any real person and listen for the answer. Let it come from you without your trying to consciously direct it – and respond. Some questions to ask might be something like:

"How are you doing?"
"How was your day? What did you do?"

In many cases, you might get the kind of answers you would expect from a dog, such as: "Oh, I hung out in the backyard," or "I had fun running around in the woods and catching balls." But in other cases, your Guide Dog might give you the kind of answers a person would, such as: "Oh, I went to your office, and I hung around the water cooler listening to what people were saying. "Accept whatever comes as part of getting acquainted.

After you break the ice, ask about whatever issue is important for you now. Ask for suggestions or images that will help you deal with whatever the situation is. For example, ask something like:

"I don't know what to do about my conflict at work with my boss. Can you give me some advice?

"I'm trying to make a hard decision now. What decision do you think I should make and why? Or can you give me a sign to know what to do?"

You can also ask your Dog Guide for specific steps to take, such as what to do next and then what to do after that to reach your goal.

Whatever your questions, whatever help you are seeking, as you get your message, write it down. You can use that input later in the real situation you have asked about. Writing it down will help you remember what to do and be more thoughtful about the suggestions you have been given. Then you can further assess how and when to use this advice, or determine if you need further information to best put this input into practice.

Getting Help on a Dog Walk

Another way to gain insights is by going on a Dog Walk with one or more of your Guide Dogs. This approach is like going on a journey to get help from a wise teacher, counselor, animal helper, or other being with knowledge. But here you are, getting insights from one of your Guide Dogs. They are like "Seeing Eye Dogs" helping you see things in new ways.

To do this Dog Walk technique, imagine yourself on local park trail walking with your Guide Dog (or team of guide dogs) to a place where you will gain new insights. You can either go with your dog or send your dog ahead to get this information and bring it back to you.

Use the following guided journey to help you on this walk. Read it first and play it back as you listen in a comfortable, relaxed state.

> *Get relaxed and imagine you are in a park or wooded area, about to walk along a trail to get an answer to a problem or issue in your life. It is a nice warm, comfortable, sunny day. You have brought along one of your Guide Dogs who you think can best help you with this issue. Or take along two or three Guide Dogs for extra help.*
>
> *Now, start walking along the path, the dogs by your side or walking a little in front of you. Let them go ahead if they want to explore or lead the way for you.*
>
> *As you walk on, think about the issue or problem you want to deal with. See it in on the horizon ahead in your mind's eye.*
>
> *Now you come to a meadow with a tall tree and a large pool of water. Go over to that tree and sit down under it, with your Guide Dog or Dogs beside you.*
>
> *Now reflect on your issue even more. As you do, tell your Guide Dog or Dogs about the problem. Explain what is especially difficult or upsetting about the situation. As you explain, your Guide Dog or Dogs listen quietly, eager to understand and show their support. Take some time now to tell them your thoughts and feelings about the problem.*
>
> *When you feel complete about what you have shared, get up with your dog or dogs and walk over to the pool of water. Then, look in the water and ask what you should do now.*

Observe what happens. You may see the answer appear in the water as an image or an object. You may hear a voice with the answer. You may see a person or animal come out of the water with information to give you.

Ask your Guide Dog or Dogs to help you get that information. For example, send your Guide Dog out to retrieve an object floating on the water. Ask it to accompany you to meet that person or animal.

Then, pay attention to whatever answer you get and ask your Guide Dog or Dogs for help in putting that answer into practice. For instance, ask your Guide Dog: "What should I do now?" and listen to the answer. Later, you can ask your Guide Dog more questions or for ongoing support as you put this advice into practice.

Putting the Advice You Get Into Action

Once you have gotten insights into what to do, the next step is to put that advice into action.

In some cases, this may involve working out a plan for what to do, and you can always turn to one of your Guide Dogs to help your planning. For example, say you realize you need to be more open and communicative with a partner. You might have a mental conversation with your Guide Dog about what to do; then write down your Guide Dog's suggestions.

Or if you already have a clear vision of what to do, you might look to your Guide Dog for support, much as you might ask a friend or spiritual helper to be with you. Say your insight is that you need to quit your job and strike out on your own by creating your own business. You might ask your Guide Dog to be with you as you take these steps. Or suppose you have called on a Bull Dog for his strength, courage, and tenacity in confronting a boss with whom you have had a difficult relationship. You might imagine the Bulldog with you as you go into your boss's office, giving you the courage to say what you really want to say, along with the thick skin to not feel upset regardless of your boss's response. Then, when you go to that meeting in reality, imagine that the Bulldog is coming with you, giving you that support, strength, and courage you need to confront your boss.

Using the Qualities of Your Guide Dog to Help

Another way to get help is to call on the Guide Dogs with the qualities you need for a particular situation.

For example, in the problem boss situation, suppose you are suddenly confronted by that boss who is angry about some problem and you have to react. If you feel a strong response is appropriate, say because your boss is unfairly accusing you of something, you might imagine that you have a tough, large, aggressive Guide Dog, giving you the strength and power to respond in a tough, firm way. Or say you feel it would be more political to take the abuse without getting personally upset, because you know your boss has a low boiling point but the problem will soon blow over if you don't react to make it worse. Then you might draw on the help of a Guide Dog who has a quality of stoic forbearance, such as a German Shepherd. In this case, you might imagine this dog there beside you, giving you the quiet strength to listen and stay calm, without getting angry.

You can also call on your Guide Dogs for help with a more personal relationship. Say you want to be more open and affectionate in your relationships, since you feel your reserve is holding you back from obtaining greater depth and intimacy. You might call on a Guide Dog with these qualities, such as a very affectionate Pomeranian or cuddly Pug, that is beside you coaching you on how to be more warm and cuddly yourself. Or perhaps imagine yourself as this Pomeranian or Pug to help you act warm and affectionate.

In short, you can call on your Guide Dog not only for advice but to help you express the qualities of this type of dog.

Some Examples of Working with Guide Dogs for Help

Here are some examples of how people have worked with Guide Dogs, drawn from workshops I conducted on working with power animals. In this program, the participants found different kinds of dogs to help them, using varied techniques.

One expressive, outgoing woman met a very playful little dog that reflected a warm, playful quality. As she described it:

"I ended up in a place where there was a small pond with trees next to it. I entered by going into the water and went through the tunnel. When I got to the end, I stepped into this place with the pond and the trees...

The animal I met was a little dog with a really long nose. It was like a cartoon character. It seemed to be always smiling, but very wise. It was running around and leaping up and down, and I felt I could really relate to it, because I could feel the excitement, too. It had this spontaneous energy. And it was very curious, eager to find out what's coming next, and very attentive. It seemed to be very independent, too...

I guess you could say those traits characterize me, too. Anyway, I liked this friendly little cartoon dog."

In this case, the woman was only trying to learn about herself by meeting her Guide Dogs, but you can also use these contacts to get information on how to deal with a particular situation in your life, as the following woman did. As her experience indicates, information may not always come to you directly, but may be in the form of symbols or signs you must interpret. At times, the information may give you guidance about some specific action to take; but at other times, the visualization or journey may be a way to release your feelings about something, so you feel a sense of completion or resolution; then there is nothing more to do.

That's what happened for one woman who had been feeling very angry about some damage she believed her neighbor did to her property. She went on a journey in which her animal helped to symbolically heal her property and take symbolic revenge on her neighbor. Afterward she felt better because she had released her negative feelings toward her neighbor.

When such negative or destructive images appear in a visualization or journey, that doesn't mean you should act on them. Rather, this experience acts as a psychological healing, which released back feelings of anger and hostility. Later, should such feelings continue to surface, you can engage in similar exercises to do more releasing.

Here's how she used a journey to express and release her long-standing anger. In this workshop, where people were invited to call on any animal for help, she imagined a gorilla coming to her aid. But if she had been calling on her Guide Dogs, she could have easily asked any of the more powerful dogs for help – such as a Great Dane. So instead of the gorilla, I have used a Great Dane in telling her story of how calling on a power animal helped.

"I went down into the tunnel, and immediately I saw this huge Great Dane, and I went up to him and asked him my question: 'How can I get revenge on my enemy?' and he said: 'Who is your enemy?' Then, I explained it was my neighbor who mutilated my oak tree while I was on vacation.

So he just beckoned to me, and I followed him, and he went up this long, long tunnel. Then we went out and across the street. I showed him the neighbor, and I could see him through his kitchen window. Then, I showed him my mutilated oak tree.

So he climbed up in the oak tree, and I realized then why I picked a Great Dane as my animal, because he was so strong, powerful, and protective. Then, he started patting the tree, as if encouraging the tree to grow.

After that, he came down and went into the neighbor's yard. Then he climbed up the neighbor's tree, and whack. He took off the top of his tree. At this point the neighbor came out, and the Great Dane took the neighbor and bashed his head open on the step, which gave me great satisfaction. Then, he went loping off up the street, waving goodbye. And he left me on my doorstep feeling gratified."

After such a journey, the next step is to interpret it. In some cases, the experience might suggest a plan of action, though here, the experience recalled a fantasy scenario of what you would like to do if you could, although realistically, you know you can't. (After all, you can't bash in the head of your neighbor, no matter how much he or she annoys you). In this case, the visualization or journey becomes a way to symbolically act out what you can't do in real life, so you can release your pent up feelings associated with the situation and move on.

The process is akin to writing an angry letter to someone, but not mailing it. The writing process gets out the anger; but you realize mailing the letter would only create worse problems, so you tear it up, and feel better for having written it.

You decide what's appropriate when you review your experience, determine what it means, and choose whether to act on it or just view it as source of insight and release. That's what the woman who got help from the Great Dane did. As she explained: "I've been puzzling and puzzling and trying to figure out what to do about my neighbor, and that's why I asked the Great Dane."But when she considered her options – from secretly going to her neighbor's property and cutting down his tree or sending in lawyers to do battle in court, she decided that it was more appropriate to consider the journey as a way of symbolically getting the revenge she had wanted to get.

Getting this symbolic revenge worked well for her because she reported that she felt better, and more satisfied seeing him and his tree injured symbolically, so she had been able to release some of her anger.

"Then, if I still feel angry in the future," she commented, "maybe I might go on a similar journey again to release more anger, and keep doing this until the anger is gone."

As she recognized, any direct real world actions against the neighbor might only inflame and escalate an already bad situation, thus using the journey in a symbolic way made the most sense, though in other cases, a journey might suggest real world options.

If you're not sure after reviewing a visualization or journey whether to take action or use it symbolically, you can always go on another journey to get clarification. To do so, simply begin your journey with the question: "Should I take some action based on my previous journey? Or should I use my journey symbolically?" Then, go to meet one of your inner Guide Dogs to learn what to do.

In other cases, your experience may suggest this isn't a question or problem to deal with now, because you can do nothing or need to wait before taking action. Sometimes your Guide Dog will tell you this directly, or if you get a jumble of confusing images or blanks, this can indicate that you should wait to act because you need to get a clearer picture of what to do.

This was the experience of a woman who turned to a Pomeranian to learn what to do about her love life. She chose a Pomeranian for help because it is a very warm, friendly, loving, affectionate dog. So what better dog to ask about love?

Unfortunately, when she asked her question and went on a journey to find the answers, she kept getting blanks and a lot of disconnected images which she didn't understand. As she reported:

"My journey didn't make any sense to me. I went back into the lower world, and when I got there, my little dog was very happy to see me. And I said: 'Here I am. I want to know about my love life and what should I do about it?'

But then, I just saw blanks for the longest time. So I thought about this one guy that I know now, and his image gradually faded away. So I began thinking that might mean I should do nothing about my love life now.

Then, I saw a street light, and I felt it was night and I thought I'll just stand on a street corner. But after I did, I wasn't getting anything. I was just standing there, and when I looked around, I saw a lot of blanks and a series of images that faded in and out. Everything seemed so disconnected.

Then, I felt it's time to go and felt unsatisfied, because I really didn't see anything. But then I said to myself, "Well, there's nothing out there, because there's nothing really you can or need to do right now.

So I guess that's what my little dog was trying to tell me. Don't do anything now. Just wait and relax. Let things happen when they will."

As these examples illustrate, when you call on your Guide Dogs in a visualization or journey, you may sometimes get direct statements advising you what to do. Or your Guide Dog may show you an image or experience, which you need to interpret, if you are not sure what this image refers to. In some cases, the advice or experience may lead you to take a particular action; in other cases it may suggest not to do anything now; and in still others it may offer a symbolic action to take in order to release your negative feelings, so you don't need to do anything more.

CHAPTER 5: PUTTING ON THE POWER DOG

Once you choose your Guide Dogs or Top Dog, you are ready to discover even more ways to work with these dogs: to unleash your creativity (pun intended!), express yourself more fully, increase your energy, relax, or just have fun. An ideal is to become more powerful by calling on or drawing on the power of a dog you consider very strong or powerful – your Power Dog for short.

While you can call on your Top Dog, Watch Dog, or Guide Dog to become a Power Dog, you can pick any dog you want to work with. Just pick on any dog that you associate with the kind of power you want at the time, whether it's the power to better perform a skill, express yourself more fully, or acquire more power in a relationship or negotiation.

While you can work with any of these techniques and exercises on your own, they are great to do with a friend, small group, or in a workshop setting. And besides being great for raising power, they're also fun.

Why These Exercises Work

These exercises are effective for several reasons.

First, from a historical perspective, they have roots deep in human culture at a time when people had a much closer kinship with animals of all types, including dogs. In many traditions around the world, dating back to the beginnings of human society and still used today, shamans have turned to animals for help and power. These techniques have their parallels with these old time techniques – though here the animal helpers are different types of dogs.

Or, for a more contemporary analogy, you might think of these exercises as much like raising excitement like a cheerleader at a football game. Or think of these exercises like raising energy at a party or celebration. As everyone gets in the spirit of the occasion, you can experience the mounting energy of the crowd and yourself surging through you. So you feel more and more power, like a charging battery.

Then, too, when you associate yourself with images and symbols of power, you draw on that power for yourself. People use everything from objects to costumes and masks to identify with and express their power. For instance, if you hold a rock or sword, put on a costume of a military leader, or put on a mask of a powerful warrior, you can feel the power of these objects transferred into you, so you experience more power. In much the same way, when you call on the help of a power animal that power surges into you.

Powering Up with Power Animals

For more information on the power of power animals, here's a historical interlude. Or skip ahead to work with these various power exercises.

When you use these different power techniques, the dogs you work with are like power animals or animal allies. Some early examples of how this works comes from ancient rock art, such as from the cave of Les Trois Frères in France, dating back to 30,000-10,000 B.C. There is the image of a half-man, half-animal creature, with a man's face and legs and a stag's antlers and tail. Sometimes it is called "the dancing sorcerer" or "le sorciere". A later image from Siberia from about 3000 B.C. shows a shaman wearing the head of a bird, and nearby a drum has two fish-like images on the canvas. Presumably, scholars believe, the shaman put on the animal mask or became the animal in a ritual in order to acquire that animal's powers.[2]

Many more recent examples show shamans, as well as others in the community, taking on the powers of different animals or transforming into these animals for a brief time in ritual. In the upper Amazon, shamans commonly turn into jaguars through singing or putting on the skin or teeth of the jaguar. In the Pacific Northwest, the Kwakiutl and other Indian groups put on the masks and skin of wolves, bears, foxes, and other powerful animals to become those animals as they dance.

In some cultures, shamans have used power animals to transport them into another spiritual world to gain insights and power from the beings or forces encountered there. For instance, the Siberian shamans ride horses or reindeer, and use drumming – or "windhorses" as they call their drums — to take them there. Other shamans use a bird to transport them into the sky or a fish to help them swim and dive in the water.[3]

The images of these animals can also be a source of power – whether during a special ritual or in everyday life. In Alaska, the Eskimo shamans carved wood or ivory animal figures as power objects; and many shamans use these objects like power charms with healing energy to help their patients.[4]

Likewise, you can use similar techniques to create a powerful working connection with any dogs you have chosen or later choose to work with. You can use these techniques on your own or incorporate them into fun group events, where you call on or become your dog with others. You are in effect putting on the dog – or more precisely, the Power Dog — to draw on that power, creativity, and spirit of self-expression for whatever you want.

---

[2] Stephen Larsen, *The Shaman's Doorway: Opening the Mythic Imagination in Contemporary Consciousness:* New York: Harper and Row, 1976, p. 6.
[3] Piers Vitebsky, *Shamanism*, University of Oklahoma Press, 201, 70.
[4] Ibid., p. 83.

A Collection of Power Exercises

Following are a series of exercises for increasing your power by working with your Power Dog. Choose whichever exercises feel most comfortable – and powerful – for you.

Dancing the Dog

This is a great exercise for raising your energy and feeling closer and more attuned with the dog you have chosen for this exercise. This also is a great technique for just exercising or having fun. While you are choosing one type of dog, if you feel so inspired, you can dance any other kind of animal. (In fact, that might be a fun experiment – try dancing a dog, a cat, or other animals and notice the difference). And if you want to do your dancing in a group, the more the merrier.

To prepare for this exercise, find a room where you can move around comfortably and listen to music.

Once the room is set up, pick a particular dog to dance. (Or in a group, each person picks their own dog). You can choose one of your dogs, your Top Dog, or whatever dog you want. The key is to choose a dog whose power you most want to access now. For example, to be more outgoing, choose a friendly, outgoing dog like a Pomeranian; to be more powerful, choose a large, powerful dog like a Great Dane.

Next, turn on some rhythmic music or play the sound of drumming in the background. (Or in a group, someone could drum or play this music).

As you listen to the music, imagine you are putting on the head or becoming the dog you are dancing. Should you have anything that represents that dog, such as a mask, fur jacket, or charm on a chain, put that on. (A fun activity that contributes to putting on your Power Dog is making these masks, jackets, or charms). If you are doing this in a group, spread out, so everyone has plenty of room for dancing their dog.

Now, as you listen to the music or drumming, feel yourself becoming more and more the dog you have chosen. Move like that dog. Imagine yourself looking at the world through that dog's eyes. Imagine your sense of smell is stronger than usual and notice any smells in the room. Notice that your hearing is keener too, so focus on all of the things you can now hear as you turn your head slowly around as you dance. Then, as your energy builds, feel free to bark or howl like that dog. Just let yourself go into the experience.

Should there be others dancing at the same time, move around and interact with one another as the dog you are each dancing. For example, move around and sniff at each other as dogs do. Hold out your hand like a paw to shake paws. Or circle each other and playfully dart forward and back, much like many dogs do when meeting at a park. Then, after a period of playful engagement, draw back and move on.

Apart from using this exercise to raise your energy generally, use it to access the type of power you associate with your chosen dog. Feel that power infusing through you and shaping the way you dance. For example, imagine you are sucking or breathing in the strength of the Great Dane, the aggressiveness of the Mastiff, the outgoing bubbly nature of the Pomeranian. Then, feel that power surge through you as something you not only feel now, but a power you can tap into when you need it, such as when you want to be more outgoing at that upcoming social event, instead of shyly hanging back as usual.

Keep dancing for 10-20 minutes, so you really feel this power and make it part of you. When you feel ready, stop dancing and turn off the music.

Afterward, take some time to relax and reflect on the experience. If you participated on your own, this is a good time to write in your journal or share your thoughts with a recorder. Or if you are experiencing this in a group, take some time to share your reactions and feelings with your partner, in a small group, or with the group as a whole.

This is a good exercise to repeat from time to time, so you continue building your connection and ability to tap into that power. Also, you can call on that animal you danced with at times when you need help. You will feel an even closer connection and feel the stronger power you need coming from that animal, because you have focused your energy on promoting a strong connection through the dance.

Relax, Relax

Say you feel jittery, nervous, or anxious about something or are wound up and want to calm down. This fun technique will help you relax – and before doing this physically, you can use the image as a reminder to calm down every day.

To prepare, find a place that's very quiet or where you can listen to soft calming music, such as environmental sounds or sitar music. Then, sit down on a comfortable chair or lie down on a couch, a bed, or pillows on the floor.

As you listen, imagine you are a dog you associate with being relaxed and lazy, such as a Beagle, Bassett Hound, or Chow Chow. Or pick a family or friend's dog that lazes around on a favorite chair, living room couch, or front porch. Then, with this relaxed dog image in mind, see yourself becoming that dog as you relax in the quiet or listen to soft music. Breathe in this dog with each breath, becoming more and more relaxed, more and more calm. Perhaps even say these words over and over to yourself as you see yourself as this dog: "I am getting more and more relaxed…I am getting more and more calm."

Continue to do this for a few minutes, until you feel completely calm and relaxed.

Later, in a tense or stressful situation, you can call on this image of yours as the dog being very relaxed to help you calm down.

One time may be enough to give you this image to use at other times. Or do this in reality several times to reinforce the experience, and later it will be a stronger image you can use. The process works like classical conditioning – you are essentially building an association between seeing the image of this laid back dog, relaxing yourself, and later using that associated image when needed to calm down.

To Unleash Your Creativity

Here's a way to have fun and become more creative by unleashing your inner dog. The process is like taking a dog off the leash in a park and letting it run free and explore. Likewise, in taking the leash off your "inner dog", you can tap into its power to try out new forms of expression in different media.

You can use any type of dog for this process, whether a Guide Dog, the dog you most like, identify with, or even a playful cartoon dog. Essentially, you imagine yourself as this dog, take off the leash, and imagine running about and exploring as this dog. You can see this in your mind's eye or on your mental screen or hold onto this image as you take part in various activities, such as running, dancing, or creating art.

Generally, it's best to imagine you are a young, playful active dog. Choose whatever breed you like, as long as you view it as having lots of energy, enthusiasm, and playfulness.

Start the process by seeing yourself as this dog in any number of ways:
- Visualize in silence or with rhythmic music that you are becoming this dog or it is becoming part of you. Perhaps imagine that you are putting on the head of this dog as part of this transformation.
- Dance as you hold this image of this dog in your head, so you dance the dog into yourself;
- Play on drums, as you imagine this dog coming toward you and stepping into you, so you become one;
- Combine any of the above activities with putting on any objects you associate with the dog you want to become – such as wearing a mask, furry jacket, or jewelry with a picture of that dog.

Once you feel you have become one with this dog, try new ways of playing with this experience. For example:

- Take a walk through your neighborhood or hike to a nearby park or beach, and look around as if you are this dog. You might sniff the flowers, jump around, and just let yourself go and enjoy. (If you are doing this with a group or are in a safe enclosed space, such as a meadow or a beach where no one else is around, try getting down on all fours or rolling around). Just think of yourself as a dog having fun and experience the enthusiasm and excitement of being that dog. (You might even try this exercise with a real dog and you become a new dog companion for your dog).
- Incorporate your experience and image of yourself as a dog in a creative project. For example, start painting or mold clay while you feel imbued with this dog spirit, and let that energy guide the process. Engage in some free form dance by yourself or with a partner as you imagine yourself as this dog. If you're with a partner, your partner can similarly imagine him or herself as a dog. Again, let this image guide you as you move in tune with the music.
- Engage in a sports activity as you imagine yourself as this dog and notice how this affects your play. For example, you are likely to have more energy, move more quickly, and be more responsive. You may experience more strength and power.

After you have imagined being a dog and expressed this feeling in any activity, reflect on your experience – on your own, with a partner, or in a group. As you reflect or share, consider how putting on the dog affected your creative process. Was there anything different about what you did, and if you did, what? Was there anything different or unique in the outcome of this creative activity, such as in your drawing or painting or in the way you danced with a partner?

Later, you can try this exercise again with the same dog or a different dog. If you do use a different dog, reflect on any differences between how you engaged in the creative process or the results.

Express Yourself More Fully

Another way to work with your inner dog is to let go to fully express yourself. Using the image of a dog for this purpose works well, because dogs are such emotion-driven creatures. They can respond with excitement or can be very laid back, because they react on a more feeling, emotional level. Since, their bodies and facial expressions reflect that emotion, you can usually quickly tell what a dog is feeling – from the happy, open mouth, and licking tongue that denote an eager, friendly dog to the bared teeth and grimace that reflect anger.

In this exercise, you'll use the image of a dog – a Guide Dog, your favorite dog, or any other dog – to help you release your feelings. Do this just for fun to express different emotions more intensely. Or if you have a particular situation where you want to express your emotions more freely – say a partner feels you are too reserved in expressing love and affection. You feel uncomfortable expressing your anger to others and want to be more assertive – you can use this exercise to deal with that issue.

To begin, pick a dog you associate with the feelings you want to express. For instance, choose a Pomeranian or Pug to express love and affection; a Great Dane to express calm authority and confidence; a Pit Bull to express aggression; a Siberian Husky to show independence and spontaneity.

Then, use one of the above techniques to identify with that dog, such as visualizing yourself putting on the dog's head of or dancing that dog. Then, by yourself or with a partner, act like that dog would in expressing feelings you want to express.

For example, say you are working on expressing love and affection as a Pomeranian. As this Pomeranian, start doing what these dogs do to show that. Hug someone, or hug an object representing that person, or visualize yourself doing this (though the more actively you can express these feelings in a physical setting the better).

Lick someone's cheek, use a round object to represent this, or visualize yourself licking someone. Bark eagerly to show how happy you are to see someone or visualize yourself doing this or come up with other things Pomeranians do. Whatever you decide to do, do it with lots of energy, excitement, and passion, just like Pomeranians.

Or say you want to be more comfortable expressing your anger rather than holding it in and are using a German Shepherd to express this. Imagine yourself as German Shepherd in a situation where you might normally express your anger, such as a police dog confronting a criminal in a large warehouse filled with boxes. A common scenario might be that you have been chasing the criminal all over the warehouse and have finally trapped him behind some large boxes, and boy, are you angry. As this German Shepherd, act or imagine yourself confronting this criminal. You could bark loudly and furiously. Bare your teeth. Snarl. Paw the ground. Arch and stiffen your back. Glare at the man with a penetrating mean gaze. In short, express all the ways you imagine a German Shepherd might express his anger. You'll find it feels good and energizing to do this. And later, when you are in a situation where you feel angry, but feel uncomfortable expressing it, think of how you did so as a German Shepherd. You'll generally feel much more assertive and able to express how you feel, if it's appropriate to do so in this situation.

If you want to experiment with experiencing a range of emotions, pick out different dogs you associate with these emotions. Then, imagine yourself putting on each of these dogs and express that emotion in various situations –physically or in your imagination, on your own, with a partner, or in a small group. If you have a particular emotion and issue to work with, pick a dog you associate with that emotion.

Increasing Your Energy

Just as you can use the image of a laid back or lazy dog to help you relax, so can you use the image of a high-energy, excited dog to help you build up your energy for whatever you are doing.

You can select the same dog to increase your energy whenever you use this exercise, or use different high-energy dogs. Or imagine yourself as part of a team of high-energy, excited dogs, upping your energy and excitement even more.

First pick a dog you think of as a high-energy dog and use a technique to identify with that dog. Then, as you imagine yourself as that dog, act to release that energy –by yourself, with a partner or in a small group. Since you are dealing with energy, act rather than try to visualize doing the exercise, though you can later use a visualization of your experience to increase your energy in everyday activities.

In deciding how to act to release that energy, let your imagination be your guide. Imagine all the things the dog you selected would do – and do them, or experience yourself as this dog in whatever activities you do. For instance:

- Run as fast as you can.
- Jump repeatedly as high as you can.
- Hop up and down on different legs.
- Chase after a stick, grab it in your teeth, and bring it back (or imagine you are grabbing it) as quickly as you can.
- As you toss balls or Frisbees back and forth, imagine you are this dog as you excitedly run to catch the ball or Frisbees.
- Find something you can climb up or over and start jumping.
- Roll around excitedly on the carpet or in the grass.
- Set up some cones or boxes in a line and run in and out of the line, just as dogs do in agility trials, going as fast as you can.
- Crawl through a doorway, under a tree in the backyard, or under a table, like a dog going through a tunnel.
- And so on.

Just think of all the things this dog might do when excited and full of energy, and do them. You'll find this technique is a real energy booster for whatever you want to do next. Also, if you're in a situation where you need energy – say a long or dull meeting – visualize your experience of raising energy. You'll immediately feel a charge of energy no matter what you are doing.

Summing Up

In sum, you can use these Power Dog techniques for various purposes – from increasing your creative abilities to better expressing your emotions to just having fun. The key techniques are the following:
- Dance the dog to feel a closer identification with the dog you have chosen to work with.
- Relax, so you become more calm, rested, and less anxious.
- Unleash your creativity by letting your inner dog run free, so you can apply it to various creative endeavors.
- Express yourself more fully, by letting your emotions run free like a dog off its leash.

ABOUT THE AUTHOR

GINI GRAHAM SCOTT, Ph.D., J.D., is a nationally known writer, consultant, speaker, and seminar leader, specializing in social trends, popular culture, business and work relationships, and professional and personal development. She has published over 50 books on diverse subjects with major publishers. She has worked with dozens of clients on memoirs, self-help, and popular business books, as well as film scripts. Her websites include www.changemakerspublishingandwriting.com and www.ginigrahamscott.com. She is a Huffington Post regular columnist, commenting on social trends, new technology, business, and everyday life at www.huffingtonpost.com/gini-graham-scott.

She is the founder of Changemakers Publishing featuring books on social trends, work, business, psychology, and self-help, which has published over 100 Print, e-books, and audiobooks. She has licensed several dozen books for foreign sales, including in the UK, Russia, Korea, Spain, Indonesia, and Japan.

She has written numerous books on creativity and visualization, including *Mind Power: Picture Your Way to Success; The Empowered Mind: How to Harness the Creative Force within You;* and *Want It, See It, Get It!*

She has received national media exposure for her books, including appearances on *Good Morning America, Oprah,* and *CNN*. She has been the producer and host of a talk show series, CHANGEMAKERS, featuring interviews on social trends.

Scott is active in a number of community and business groups, including the Lafayette, Danville, and Pleasant Hill Chambers of Commerce. She is a graduate of the prestigious Leadership in Contra Costa County program and is a member of a BNI group in Walnut Creek, B2B groups in Danville and Walnut Creek, and many other business networking groups. She is the organizer of six Meetup groups in the film and publishing industries with over 6000 members in Los Angeles and the San Francisco Bay Area. She also does workshops and seminars on the topics of her books.

She received her Ph.D. from the University of California, Berkeley, and her J.D. from the University of San Francisco Law School. She has received five MAs at Cal State, East Bay, including most recently an MA in Communications. She will be starting an additional MA program in history there in the fall of 2017.

CHANGEMAKERS PUBLISHING
3527 Mt. Diablo Blvd., #273
Lafayette, CA 94549
changemakers@pacbell.net . (925) 385-0608
www.changemakerspublishingandwriting.com

www.ingramcontent.com/pod-product-compliance
Lightning Source LLC
Chambersburg PA
CBHW071534080526
44588CB00011B/1665